GLOUCESTER'S

Sea Serpent

WAYNE SOINI

GLOUCESTER'S
Sea Serpent

WAYNE SOINI

THE
History
PRESS

Published by The History Press
Charleston, SC 29403
www.historypress.net

Front cover image: Courtesy of the Cape Ann Museum, Gloucester, Massachusetts.
Back cover images: Photo by Manuel Simoes; illustration courtesy of the Cape Ann
Museum.

First published 2010

Manufactured in the United States

ISBN 978.1.59629.461.5

Library of Congress Cataloging-in-Publication Data

Soini, Wayne, 1948-
Gloucester's sea serpent / Wayne Soini.
p. cm.
Includes bibliographical references.
ISBN 978-1-59629-461-5
1. Sea monsters--Massachusetts--Gloucester--History--19th century. 2. Gloucester
(Mass.)--History--19th century. I. Title.
QL89.2.S4S65 2010
001.944--dc22
2010036878

To my parents, Waino and Florence Soini;
to the volunteers and staff of the Cape Ann Museum, past and present;
to Gloucester harbor;
and to the sea serpent of 1817, without any of whom, there would be no book!

There are more things in heaven and earth, Horatio,
Than are dreamt of in your philosophy.
Hamlet, *I. i:166–67*

CONTENTS

ACKNOWLEDGEMENTS

Blanche Dubois, who all of her life relied on the kindness of strangers, was only half right; we rely on the kindness of those whom we know, too. In books, as in life, helpful people are half of the time anonymous and half of the time known by name.

Among these latter type saints, I should like to acknowledge Anne, my partner, and children Eric, Heather and Kevin; my fifth-grade teacher, Mr. Paul T. Harling, for having introduced me to the sea serpent; John D. Cunningham III, Esq., of Cunningham & Cunningham, who stood with me in Mr. Harling's class in 1958 at the Cape Ann Museum, over which he currently and brilliantly presides; my first English teacher—unfortunately, posthumously—Miss Helen Cohen of the old Central Grammar School, who selected me to be the first class secretary one academic year long ago, and who would certainly have told me of this book, "I knew that you could do it!"; two timely and exemplary mentors, English professor Charlotte Spivack of the University of Massachusetts–Amherst and history professor Julie Winch of the University of Massachusetts–Boston; the late Howard V. Doyle, president–director of AFSCME Council 41, AFL-CIO and Angelo A. Amato, Council 41's longtime secretary, who offered me my first paid writing job; the indefatigable Stephanie Buck, archivist and librarian of the Cape Ann Museum; Gloucester salts Peter Prybot, David Rose and his brother, and Gloucester harbormaster Jim Caulkett; Kathryn Glenn, the North Shore coordinator of the Massachusetts Office of Coastal Zone Management; my late grandfather, the master mariner and unpublished but prolific poet and author, Captain Chester L. Morrissey; the amiable and generous encourager of authors, Gary K. Wolf, creator of "Roger Rabbit"; Harvard professor George C. Lodge, whose great-great-great-great-grandfather was Judge John Davis; the lively Boston chapter of the National Writers Union headed by co-chairs Charles Coe and Barbara Beckwith; the late Fred J. Kyrouz, one of Lonson Nash's successors as Gloucester justice of the peace, unique, personable and charismatic; patient editors Jeffrey Saraceno and Amber Allen and the rest of the staff of The History Press; and, last but not least, the wonderful man who provides my day job, James V. DiPaola, sheriff of Middlesex County.

For those whom I've named and the many people who helped me anonymously along the way, THANKS is too small a word, even written in capital letters!

INTRODUCTION

This is the story of people who passed the torch of science in their own lifetimes and who, to this day, shed light on another species of life. It recounts how, in frail little crafts made of nothing more than paper and ink, the people of Gloucester in 1817 caught the biggest "fish" of all—the sea serpent.

Gloucester's sea serpent of 1817 was a puzzle, a project and a flop.

He—none of the Gloucester eyewitnesses called the sea serpent "it," but always "he"—was a puzzle because God made him that way; a project because Judge John Davis wanted his Linnaean Society of New England to have the honor of naming the sea serpent; and a flop because a Loblolly Cove snake distracted and confused the judge and his committee, who then lost their chance at international scientific acclaim.

Puzzle, project or flop, the sea serpent may still be seen in Gloucester.

I first sighted him, and the reader may, too, at the Cape Ann Museum on Pleasant Street in Gloucester, formerly the home of Captain Elias Davis. There, in the large bric-a-brac room on the mansion's second floor, a volunteer told us about the mystery.

Looking closely into the upturned faces of the fifth-graders at Mr. Paul T. Harling's Beeman Memorial School on a field trip—with a sustained eye contact that would have been impolite under other circumstances—our volunteer generated suspense as she spoke with a deliberate and delicious slowness. Without a hint that any of this happened earlier than the previous week, she said that many Gloucester people claimed to have seen a sea

The Cape Ann Museum, 27 Pleasant Street in Gloucester, formerly the home of Captain Elias Davis and built in 1804, is seen in a photograph circa 1925. *Courtesy of the Cape Ann Museum.*

The Cape Ann Museum, circa 1980, in a photograph by Jean Baer O'Gorman. *Courtesy of the Cape Ann Museum.*

An 1817 engraving of Gloucester's sea serpent. This is only one of several made by imaginative artists at the time that were placed on public display in Boston for an admission fee. The central figure, in fact, bears no resemblance to the sea serpent as described by eyewitnesses. *Courtesy of the Cape Ann Museum.*

serpent. After naming people like Amos Story, Mrs. Story, James Mansfield, William Foster and Matthew Gaffney and summarizing their statements, her climax was visual and dramatic. Turning, she pointed out to us the serpentine suspect—still swimming, framed behind glass as a golden dragon with a horn and scales! Well, that was it; when she asked us to raise our hands to vote on whether we thought a sea serpent actually visited Gloucester in 1817, we all voted no.

But a little knowledge is a dangerous thing.

I have long pondered that engraving. I conclude that it is one of several imaginative products intended to satisfy consumer wants but not actual needs (some things never change). A very traditional sea monster, like those that have swam in the margins of maps since before Christopher Columbus's time, it was simply drawn to draw in the people P.T. Barnum said were born one a minute.

May I demonstrate?

Ladies and gentlemen, anybody ought to recognize a carnival barker cadence; grandiloquent, rhetorical and amusing tropes that to this day continue to delight more than to inform, from the producer of just such an engraving, a man who devoted his life—as the hangman said on the day of a public execution—to gather a crowd. Step right up and see exactly what I mean, folks, in an advertisement in print for the first time in almost two centuries; one that dates back to the days of President James Monroe, from the happy days of the first year of the Era of Good Feelings, the year of the sea serpent himself, the year, my friends—and only as long as it lasted—1817:

The Sea Serpent
  A Monster of Uncommon Size
  Who has paid a long visit to our eastern coast and has excited the admiration of scientific men, and the western world in general, has been accurately painted by an artist of the first talents, under the direction of a gentleman, whose genius and minute observation of the monster entitle him to the confidence of the public! and now exhibiting at

UNION HOTEL, 68 William Street on upward of three hundred square feet of canvass.
  PRICE OF ADMITTANCE, 25 CENTS.
  The Painting of this wonderful animal, which is now exhibited at Washington Hall, is, in many respects, one of the most interesting displays ever presented to the public. It covers a canvass about 35 feet by 20, representing a beautiful view of a bay opening to the ocean, with boats, vessels, and hills, in the distance, and the Serpent stretching his enormous and formidable length across the front. The painting is well executed, and every object in it—and the land, waves, vessels, clouds, sky, light and shade, so justly arranged as to please the taste of general beholders. When we consider that the principal design is to give the public a correct idea of a terrible animal which is now known to exist, as it were, in the neighborhood of our city, which appalls the courage and baffles the skill of everyone attempting its approach, we feel fully warranted in asserting, that it is a spectacle so magnificent, so sublime, as to be surpassed only by the awful monster which it represents. The interest of the spectator is increased by the consideration that there is no fancy, no fiction, and no poetry in the view—but that it is only a PENCIL DISPLAY of a monster whose force is irresistible, whose movement is swift as the wind, and the terror of whose eye can no more be painted than the strength, the swiftness, or the noise of his movements over the ocean waves.
  The views are taken from the representations of a celebrated naturalist whose enterprising vigilance has given him an opportunity, six different

times, to approach so near the animal as to see his eyes, teeth, tongue, and the color of his head and neck, distinctly. We may therefore look on the painting as a fact, and contemplate the animal, with his lofty head erect in the air, and his long and spiral volumes dashing over the waves as a moving miracle, bearing down stubborn incredulity and oppressing the beholder with the weight of the most "TERRIBLE" and the most "SUBLIME." In all the arts there is nothing like the painting—for the academicians never knew of any thing in nature like the SEA SERPENT; and every AMERICAN should be proud that we are the first to give this interesting subject of the pencil a SHAPE AND FORM.

At Suffolk University Law School, I learned to weigh the testimony of witnesses by factors like consistency, corroboration and probability, and, at the University of Massachusetts–Boston recently, how to read documents like the proverbial porcupine—very carefully. Having very carefully read and weighed testimony, I have overcome the engraving that still hangs in the museum. If I could only find our volunteer and she would allow me to change my vote, I would officially free myself to try and persuade the reader that Gloucester was indeed visited by a sea serpent in August 1817.

Proceeding unofficially in that task anyway, I am ably assisted, albeit posthumously, by the Honorable John Davis, one of President John Adams's "Midnight Judges" of 1801. Unlike our museum volunteer, the judge rejected all engravings of the sea serpent swimming in Gloucester harbor as evidence in his scientific book. Even so, his book, with its appropriately serpentine title, the *Report of a Committee of the Linnaean Society of New England Relative to a Large Marine Animal, Supposed to be a Serpent, Seen near Cape Ann, Massachusetts, in August, 1817*, by Judge Davis, Francis C. Gray and Jacob Bigelow, MD, was published only once. His Honor's mistake was a snake. The judge and his committee stumbled over a snake from Loblolly Cove (today part of Rockport, near the Gloucester line) that a local farmer pierced through with his pitchfork while it was minding its own slow business and crawling through his salt hayfield. Convinced that it was no coincidence but kindred of the sea serpent, the judge included an accurate, very carefully engraved drawing of the dissected snake in his book. Having wiggled its way from a hayfield into history, that little snake cost the judge and his committee their place in American science and allowed the elusive sea serpent—the dragon of the seas, the biblical leviathan—to escape from his intended classifiers.

And yet, did he escape?

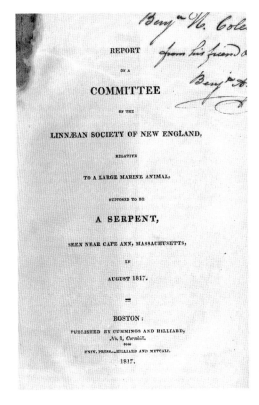

REPORT

OF A

COMMITTEE

OF THE

LINNÆAN SOCIETY OF NEW ENGLAND,

RELATIVE

TO A LARGE MARINE ANIMAL,

SUPPOSED TO BE

A SERPENT,

SEEN NEAR CAPE ANN, MASSACHUSETTS,

IN

AUGUST 1817.

═

BOSTON:

PUBLISHED BY CUMMINGS AND HILLIARD,
No. 1, Cornhill.

UNIV. PRESS...HILLIARD AND METCALF.

1817.

The title page of one of the rarest scientific books in the United States: Judge Davis's book on the sea serpent. His *Report of a Committee of the Linnaean Society of New England relative to a Large Marine Animal, Supposed to be a Serpent, Seen near Cape Ann, Massachusetts, in August, 1817* includes the full text of all depositions taken in August 1817 by Justice Nash. *Courtesy of the Cape Ann Museum.*

Well, in part, he certainly did. The sea serpent that visited Gloucester in August 1817 remains an enormous void, full of mystery still. I do not pretend that, if readers will separate the serious from the silly and the serpent from the snake, they may pin the big guy down. All I say is that Judge Davis's book has value, as does the C.L. Sargent manuscript. I owe the C.L. Sargent manuscript to Stephanie Buck, archivist and librarian, at the Cape Ann Museum, who unearthed and invited my attention to one of the Cape Ann Museum's rarest curiosities. On its face a handwritten and flimsy notebook of a few pages, the C.L. Sargent manuscript is, in fact, an original available nowhere else and the best primary source of information on the sea serpent. Previously published only in part and richer in several ways than the depositions of Judge Davis's book, it is the proof that every trial lawyer hopes for, namely, independent corroborating evidence. In his notebook in 1818, Gloucester-born captain Charles Lenox Sargent preserved the recollections of sixteen witnesses never interviewed for Judge Davis's book.

A word of warning is nonetheless in order: even with Judge Davis and his book and C.L. Sargent and his manuscript, the readers' knowledge of Gloucester's sea serpent, like mine, will always remain incomplete. Gnawing questions persist. For instance, why did the sea serpent stay so long in Gloucester harbor in August 1817? Why did he act as if he were a trained part of the show at SeaWorld rather than a marine animal in

A retired and probably sickly captain of the merchant service, Charles Lenox "C.L." Sargent made notes of sightings by Gloucester men and women who were not interviewed by Judge Davis's committee. Although he probably intended that the sea serpent would be the theme of his third book, Captain Sargent died before he could do more than write up summaries of sightings. *Courtesy of the Cape Ann Museum.*

the wild? Gloucester's sea serpent, swimming in and around the land-girt harbor of the populated town for three weeks, splashed about as the world's most gregarious sea serpent ever, one that seemed to thrive on attention. Gloucester's pinwheeling pet clocked more hours with human beings than all earlier-reported sea serpents that had flopped into fjords or swum by ships at a distance, taken altogether. At bottom, the happy visitor's extended stay in Gloucester, even in August, remains an unfathomable mystery.

Then there was the attempt to kill him. Just once—just one shot. Ship carpenter Matthew Gaffney's single shot on the eventful day of August 14, 1817, is fraught with frustration for a historian. What was it all about? What exactly happened before, during and after the shot? Questions abound about what Gaffney intended; why others did not shoot; why Gaffney stopped after one shot; and how it was that Gaffney, an experienced marksman, missed, or, if he did not miss, how it was that the sea serpent stayed and played on with no obvious injury? To paraphrase Winston Churchill: some shot, some sea serpent!

All of them, Gloucester's Matthew Gaffney, the Midnight Judge and his fellow committee members, Gloucester author and sea captain C.L. Sargent, Gloucester's justice of the peace Lonson Nash and the Gloucester woman who was surely the love of his life, Nabby (Lowe) Nash, are only sketched or side-profiled here because documents do not survive for the full-length portraits they all deserve. Hints of unexplored drama hover in the corners of existing documents including circumstantial but fairly strong evidence that the arc of Lonson Nash's life reached its height upon his connection with the sea serpent, after which it was all downhill.

But the reader doubtless did not buy or borrow this book to solve such mysteries. First and last, the reader's chief question is assumed to be the same one that the volunteer asked us fifth-graders: whether a sea serpent actually visited Gloucester in 1817.

To that end, Gloucester mariners, captains and merchants, skilled laborers, housewives, ropewalkers, folks at the harbor windmills and a scared teenager in a rowboat at night speak here exactly as they once spoke, each in turn, either to Justice Nash in 1817 or to C.L. Sargent in 1818. When the reader is done with the book, then he or she is invited to cast his or her secret ballot, yes or no.

Did he really visit Gloucester harbor in August 1817, a sea serpent that swam circles around sailboats in the sunshine, his chocolate-brown body incredibly long and so marvelously flexible that he could come and go at the same time; a creature that sunbathed on the beach on Ten Pound Island but, in Gloucester harbor, zipped past awestruck onlookers doing four-minute miles, with his head flat at the top and pointed like a serpent with bulges at the sides and a tongue that he could flip up and drop back at whim; a sea serpent that, when paired with her putative baby in Judge Davis's book, became incredible; a sea serpent prevented by that little snake from being accepted and recognized until—just now?

Chapter 1

JUSTICE NASH
ON THE EDGE

Lonson Nash, a graduate of Williams College who was certainly one of the best-educated and best-read men of Gloucester, probably had been idly curious. In the right time and at the right place, in Gloucester on August 14, 1817, Nash, along with many others, covered the waterfront. For his part, Nash went to Stage Fort to see the sea serpent. While others sailed and rowed in the harbor, Nash was peering through a "glass," or telescope. Assuming that Nabby and the children were not with the justice as he stood among rowdy mariners, when he went home he had a tale to tell—one that he doubtless never thought would either be published or affect his life. But he was wrong on both counts. Nash was soon drafted to help with a book on Gloucester's sea serpent by a small committee in Boston headed by Justice Nash's friend and Federalist political ally, Judge John Davis. And the sea serpent's brief, sudden appearance made ripples in Nash's future for years.

Scanning the harbor's deep waters for a disturbance, Nash took a break from watching Gloucester and the United States during a disturbing time. Nash, a man of a conservative nature politically and socially, who married once for life and who remained loyal to the Federalist Party until it died before he did, was normally the classic man of status quo. It was Gloucester and the United States that had slipped their moorings and were adrift. The Gloucester from which Nash stared out into the waves was not the Gloucester he had set foot on some ten years earlier. In the decade since Nash had arrived in Gloucester from western Massachusetts in 1806—back when Essex County was the political epicenter of Federalism nationally—

the Federalist tide had been going out. To be a Federalist in 1817, as Nash remained with dogged stubbornness, was to be a Federalist as the party's flame was sputtering. The erstwhile dominant party that had made John Adams the country's second president, the party that had controlled state legislatures and that, in turn, controlled the election of United States senators, the once-mighty Federalists—Lonson Nash among them—stood on the edge of darkness.

Gloucester was vulnerable to outside events because, by 1812, the town was not the farming village it had been a century earlier. The White–Ellery House, circa 1710, owned and maintained today by the Cape Ann Museum, mirrors that earlier time and stands a vestige and an example of days when Gloucester's settlers farmed for a living in their corner of Massachusetts. Before residents built that parsonage for Reverend John White on the marshy edge of the Annisquam River, the "Cut," known today as the Blynman

Before the "Cut," the center of Gloucester was not its harbor but a cluster of subsistence farms that are today only so many cellar-holes in wooded "Dogtown Common." In order to recruit a full-time minister to Gloucester, the community built a "saltbox"-style Colonial house in about 1710. Reverend White moved in, succeeded by the prolific Ellery family, members of whom lived in the house through the twentieth century. The White–Ellery House, pictured here as it was in about 1895, is now owned and operated by the Cape Ann Museum. *Courtesy of the Cape Ann Museum.*

Canal, had linked the harbor to the river. When, beginning in the 1640s, what had been a peninsula was turned into an island and the harbor became a rotary, boats "out o' Gloucester" could—and did—go as easily around the world as around the Cape; and fishing and trade increasingly supplemented farming income until Gloucester people made their living off the sea. The string of subsistence farms, like spokes on a wheel emanating from the Town Green (today's Grant Circle), were abandoned to the dogs and became "Dogtown." Not only fishermen, shipowners, merchants, captains and crews but also boat builders, ship chandlers, sail loft workers, coopers, ropewalk operators, cartwrights, teamsters and laborers found profitable places as goods and fish streamed in and out of Gloucester harbor.

Thomas Jefferson's Embargo Act had obstructed trade for years and, once war was declared, Gloucester's whole fleet stood idle, soon fouled by barnacles and sea clams, at anchorage as trade stopped and fishing ceased. The British navy controlled the seas. On land, the British burned the White House. With impunity, a passing British frigate shot a cannonball that struck the steeple of the First Parish (Congregational) church in the center of Middle Street, a block back from Gloucester's waterfront. All along the exposed New England coast, the Federalist Party rose up to be America's first peace activists. Judging the war to be a mistake, the Federalists offered many arguments but one especially impressed Gloucester voters, who passed a resolution in June 1812 that urged its state government to take measures "to break in pieces the chains prepared to bind us to the car of the Corsican"— Napoleon. The war was a French plot to ruin the United States.

Antiwar protests spilled out into Boston streets as delegates from over fifty town meetings, including Gloucester's senator Lonson Nash, met to name three "peace ambassadors" to lobby Congress. The Federalist governor of Massachusetts, Caleb Strong, sent secret word to England that he was willing to broker a separate peace. Meeting behind closed doors in Hartford from December 1814 through January 1815, party leaders planned to secede just before Andrew Jackson's victory at New Orleans. The war was suddenly over and America had won. Peace was, for the peace party, an unmitigated catastrophe. The War of 1812 literally tore the Federalist Party apart. After 1816, Federalists no longer ran candidates for president but, rather, shrank state by state into smaller and smaller enclaves of local politicians. With exceptions up and down the coast, Federalist lights were going out all over the country. Gloucester was not one of the coastal exceptions. Among the Federalist casualties of peace was Lonson Nash. His political successes turned to ashes; he had no political future.

The Unitarian Church on Middle Street in Gloucester, seen here in an 1870s photograph, was built over the site of the First Parish (Congregational), which was hit by a cannonball fired from a British frigate off Norman's Woe during the War of 1812. *Courtesy of the Cape Ann Museum.*

Outside Gloucester, famine, plague and disorder, those other Horsemen of the Apocalypse, rode globally as crops failed, sheep and cattle perished and people fell under onslaughts of unremitting and unprecedented cold and wet weather that followed from an Indonesian volcano. In April 1815 Mount Tambora blew up. Calculated at the top of the Volcanic Explosivity Index to be a seven—unequalled to this day (Mount Saint Helens in 1980 was a five)—its ear-shattering initial explosion was heard a thousand miles away. Molten lava, tsunamis, rolling waves of poisonous gases and clouds of burning ash killed tens of thousands. Five-square-mile rafts of pumice drifted over the Pacific. More devastating than any war, a tall plume of fine ash from the largest eruption since earth's prehistory punched through the stratosphere, darkened the globe and, the following year, evenly dispersed billions of tiny sulfur particles that reflected sunlight back into space, making 1816 "the year without a summer."

In Virginia, former president and eternal intellectual Thomas Jefferson coolly noted falling temperatures at Monticello. Jefferson's "table of thermometrical observations" from January 1, 1810, to December 31, 1816, now at the Library of Congress, permits comparison of the summer of 1816 against the mean temperatures and range of temperatures for the same months of 1810 through 1816. Compared to an overall mean for June of seventy-two degrees Fahrenheit, the mean for June 1816 at Monticello was seventy, including the lowest June temperature in seven years, fifty-one; July 1816's mean was a low seventy-five, with another seven-year low of seventy-one; in August 1816, temperatures surged upward only touching average. These fifties-to-low-seventies temperatures in Virginia equated with frost and summer snow in Canada and New England. In 1816, Quebec City was buried under a foot of snow in mid-June. Each month, New England was hard hit somewhere by frost. A series of deadly, surprise frosts at higher elevations interrupted food production on New England farms, as they did across the ocean. Around the hard-hit, already war-shattered Mediterranean, epidemics decimated Italian, French and Spanish villages, and starving people rioted only to be brutally suppressed by panicked authorities.

As the world seemed to be in its last days, literature went nightmarish.

Mary Shelley, a teenager on holiday during the bleak and stormy summer of 1816, stayed indoors and began to write a horror story that showcased the futility of human progress. Completed and published in 1818 as *Frankenstein, the Modern Prometheus*, her novel reflected a planet spinning out of control, a gift of Mount Tambora's violence, and Frankenstein drifting out to sea on ice.

The first vampire novel, *Vampyre* by John Polidori, came out in 1819.

Readers were given a little hope of help from nature, but only a little, in the long poem that Samuel Taylor Coleridge presciently revived in 1817, his weird and hallucinatory *Rime of the Ancient Mariner*. A pantheistic coronation of nature as God, the poem is hardly less nightmarish than *Frankenstein*, for in Coleridge's vision, all of a ship's crew die but one. The curse stops just short of the proud hunter who had shot the ship's good-luck escort, an albatross; just in time, the albatross drops from his neck when he sees that even "slimy things" of the "slimy seas" are beautiful. Its moral was obvious and in line with *Frankenstein* and the famous television commercial of our time: "It isn't nice to mess with Mother Nature." Several authors, in a synchrony of zeitgeist, made 1817 the perfect time for a sea monster to appear with the maximum chance of being considered beautiful and of being left alone.

Nonetheless, as chaos reigned and rained down upon the earth, as Nash's party collapsed, as Gloucester sailors slowly got their sea legs back and as Gloucester's merchants cautiously began to cast their bread upon the waters, a letter from Judge Davis interrupted whatever Nash was planning or doing. Suddenly feeling less isolated on the edge of the North American continent and after considering the potential risks either not at all or hastily discounting them, Nash welcomed the unusual summons. Sensing that he was in the right place at the right time for a purpose, he cheerfully signed up to help. Only someone who knew their Coleridge very well would have shuddered at the hazards that lay ahead.

Chapter 2
JOHN JOSSELYN'S
"QUOILED SNAKE" REVISITED

W as 1817 the first time that a sea serpent appeared in Cape Ann? John Josselyn made notes in New England in the 1600s, notes that he sorted out and published in his old age. Apart from his name and his putative occupation (he is thought to be a physician or surgeon), we know that Josselyn seems to have been an extravert with a network of friends in England, where he lived for most of his life. If he was married, if he ever fathered children, how well he loved his parents or whether he acquired a taste for tobacco and enjoyed warm beer, Josselyn never set it to words. But, as is obvious from his books, for Josselyn New England was a living zoo and botanical garden to which he was drawn, incredibly, twice. Josselyn endured dangers and hardships, he said, to see his brother once and to run a new hymnal of psalms translated from Hebrew to a Puritan minister in Boston another time. Such were the cover stories for stays in New England during which he took aim with his pen at New England wildlife, including a sea serpent.

Josselyn, all eyes for new plants and animals, was all ears, too. His long lists of Indian names and catalogue of New Englanders' various names for plants and animals reflect leisurely conversations. Josselyn was regaled by a tale of the Cape Ann sea serpent in the early summer of 1638.

His diary entry ran as follows:

> *June the Six and twentieth day, very stormie, Lightning and Thunder. I heard now two of the greatest and fearfullest thunderclaps that ever were heard, I am confident. At this time we had some neighboring Gentlemen*

in our house who came to welcome me into the Countrey; where amongst variety of discourse they told me of a young Lyon (not long before) kill'd at Piscataway by an Indian, of a Sea-Serpent or Snake, that lay quoiled up like a Cable upon a Rock at Cape-Ann; a Boat passing by with English aboard, and two Indians, they would have shot the Serpent, but the Indians dissuaded them, saying, that if he were not kill'd outright, they would be all in danger of their lives.

Because Josselyn neither identified the rock nor dated the year of that original sighting more precisely, no rock among the rocks of Cape Ann's shores has been singled out and engraved with a year in raised letters as "Sea Serpent Rock," memorializing where the sea serpent landed.

Josselyn's tale is, of course, suspect as a fictional composite because a sea serpent coiled like a snake on a rock sounds more like a reptile than a marine mammal. Nonetheless, Josselyn's anonymous hearsay is worth reading—very carefully.

Putting aside the tale's slithering snakiness, its underlying structure is of English and Indian interaction. An unstated number of Englishmen and two Indians (as Native Americans were then known) were traveling together. Probably a handful of armed Englishmen with two armed Indians, presumably their guides, were exploring the New England coastline and incidentally hunting, or perhaps they were hunting and incidentally exploring. Presumably, the Englishmen left behind their large ocean-crossing vessel in favor of a pinnace with a sail, a ship's longboat or maybe even a sea-going canoe—in any case certainly a small craft that they kept close to shore. When the Englishmen began the time-consuming and slow process of loading their blunderbusses or raising ready muskets to their shoulders or on a tripod preparatory to taking a shot, the boat they were in mattered. The Indians were in the same boat. Thus, they did not look on with indifference and instantly protested—but their intervention was too strong to be warranted by a distant rock-hugging snake, however large. Instead, several men in a tub facing a strong and sizeable maritime monster in the water near enough to be within range of old-time firearms would have presented the life-threatening danger.

Detailed analysis supports this point.

The Indians said that if the sea serpent "were not killed outright, they would all be in danger of their lives." The quotation must be understood as summary, if not an inadequate surmise, of what any Indian said. English-speaking explorers, traders and settlers dealt with Native Americans without bilingual schools or qualified translators. In other words, how much English did these Indians know before 1638? Or, how much Algonquian did the English voyagers know before (or after) 1638? In all likelihood, a limited, if not profane, vocabulary or vigorous gestures constituted the Indians' assertion of authority over Englishmen in order to prevent a catastrophe at sea.

Who told the story to Josselyn?

Who told the story to Josselyn's informant?

It is impossible to know but, on its face again, the story is a peculiar kind of story for an English "Gentleman" to tell—an episode in which Indian wisdom is celebrated. It makes sense to ask why a story about Indians knowing more than the greenhorn Englishmen was told and by whom. The story, with substantial probability, began its life as an Indian guide commercial, a story circulated by Indians not too shy to step forward to tell potential customers about Indian prowess and persuasive life-saving advice in the face of danger, during retellings of which a "coiled snake on a rock" centerpiece evolved.

How did the serpent come to be coiled on a rock in the telling before it reached Josselyn? Perhaps an Indian once indicated the serpent's undulating course or humps with hand gestures. Was he then misunderstood to mean that the sea serpent coiled up? Or did the Indian mimic a coil-like gesture that embodied such a sea serpent maneuver on water? In 1817, witnesses in Gloucester saw the sea serpent coil back upon itself in water.

At bottom, Josselyn published an internally contradictory account of a large, strong marine animal feared by Indians at sea while it was coiled or sluggishly sunning itself on a rock. Josselyn's fish out of water was fiction, nothing to believe in, let alone to fear, although the other tongue of the story, the imperative to kill a sea serpent and not just to wound "him," sounds like authentic Indian lore—curiously even including the masculine pronoun "him" rather than "it."

Josselyn's report remains garbled proof that the Native Americans in or near Cape Ann were familiar with the sight (and, apparently, the taste) of sea serpents which they warily hunted off-shore before 1638. It can be contrasted against accounts in Gloucester in 1817, when a sea serpent was no longer consigned to be the brief and garbled anecdote of an anonymous Indian guide or the casual recollection of an English crewman passing time with a British tourist at a tavern before a fireside. This time would be lastingly different because of Judge Davis—and his friend, Justice Nash.

Chapter 3
HERE COMES THE JUDGE!

The judge came; the judge wrote; the judge published a book. He headed the region's most elite amateur scientific establishment, a gentlemen's Saturday-meeting club headquartered in Boston, the Linnaean Society of New England. Like their rented museum of plants, animals and rocks from all over the world, the members' interests embraced all fields of science. The natural question is this: what on earth (or at sea) led Judge Davis to publish on the risky topic of the sea serpent?

It is documented that, on short notice just as suddenly as a sea serpent appeared in Gloucester, Judge Davis immediately recruited two busy, unpaid volunteers to join him for this project. He also reached out to Justice Nash, his political ally, for help, although Nash was neither a member nor a scientist. As will be detailed, Judge Davis cleared his schedule to interview crew members of the *Laura* in Boston, with resulting affidavits signed by them. Besides those interviews, he soon entered into correspondence and dusted off volumes of French scientists, researching the context of a possible book. At greater leisure, Judge Davis dedicated time to organizing reports of the Gloucester sightings forwarded by Justice Nash. His involvement was unceasing; his energy unflagging. He finally either funded publication of the book himself or raised funds for the book, privately published in the Linnaean Society's name. Unwaveringly, for more than a year from first report through publication of the book, his own name prominent as both the president of the Society and chairman of the committee, Judge Davis made a huge bet on the success of his Gloucester sea serpent project. It is clear that he staked his own and his group's reputation ultimately on the credibility of a legendary creature, the sea serpent. When his project failed, so did the Linnaean Society of New England. This much is traceable. But that narrative of history does not answer the most natural question: why did Judge Davis take such a gamble?

Little survives from which to reconstruct Judge John Davis's motives for spearheading a sea-serpent project. No newspaper interviews, letters or diary entries explain why Judge Davis (not to be confused with a later John Davis, a younger politician twice elected as governor of Massachusetts) would head a sea-serpent committee, and why he would further recruit two friends to join him.

On the other hand, not one but several competing factors suggest themselves: his Plymouth connection, America's ongoing cultural war with France, Davis's intellectual curiosity or—bizarre as it might sound—revenge on Thomas Jefferson.

Plymouth, where John Davis was born and raised, may have figured if Davis grew up hearing reports of sea serpents in that seaport, making him immune against skepticism. In pinball fashion, in his mind as later in his book, South Shore sightings served to support the credibility of the Cape Ann creature. When he wanted a recent sighting to compare against Gloucester's sea serpent, Judge Davis sent to Plymouth for one. His brother returned a sworn statement by Captain Elkanah Finney that went into Judge Davis's book.

Was France the motivator? The United States had just defended its political independence by defeating Great Britain but, to become culturally independent, it was unquestionably France that the country had to take on. Davis himself read French and Latin, Buffon and Linnaeas. He well knew that French scientists followed the late Count Buffon, who argued that European animals were always bigger, stronger, smarter, etc., than their North American equivalents. The same Buffon Theory had motivated Jefferson, as soon as he made the Louisiana Purchase, to order Lewis and Clark to bring back a mammoth. Where Jefferson, Lewis and Clark and others had failed, Judge Davis could succeed. In 1817, the discovery of a huge marine animal in North America—longer, more flexible, faster and stronger than any whale—would strike Paris like a lightning bolt. All of his life, Judge Davis literally held in his hand constant evidence of French success in the cultural wars, as his scientific literature, books in French, arrived by ship. Now traffic could go the other way in a book by the Linnaean Society of New England. Thus, a patriotic mission beckoned from Cape Ann. With a sea serpent, Judge Davis could command the attention of the world to the bounties of American nature and, incidentally, to the brilliance of amateur American scientists. The sea serpent treading water at the country's doorstep could make the American case. American science could come of age. A sea change was at hand or, if you will, at fin.

Or was Davis's curiosity behind all of this? The man from Plymouth whose specialty was finance and treasury matters—he quit being President Washington's comptroller because the job did not pay enough—was also the history buff who named the original settlers of Plymouth "the pilgrims." Davis—in Plymouth, at Harvard during the Revolution, in Washington, as United States attorney and on the bench in Boston—had always led two lives. The sharp-eyed money cruncher was also the wide-eyed curious intellectual. The streetwise politician, skillful bureaucrat and judicious Federal judge wrote poems, told stories, read books and made notes in English and in French. Judge Davis rented a pew to the left of the pulpit at the front of the Federal Street Congregational Church, where he could be observed making notes to preserve the sermon. What would a man who made notes in church do when a sea serpent appeared?

Finally, was it Jefferson? When Judge Davis considered scientific competitors, he looked south to the country's best-known amateur scientist. Jefferson's only book, *Notes on Virginia*, was a philomath's book of history, geology, topography and other disciplines. When Jefferson was first elected president—president of the American Philosophical Society, which included scientists in all fields—a wild flower, a sort of daisy, *Jeffersonia binata*, was immediately named in his honor. Jefferson turned his Virginia home into a museum of natural oddities. Guests who entered his front door had to run a gauntlet between huge claws and bones, the toothy jaw of a mastodon and the arching horns of a gigantic musk ox that someone had dug up in the West and sent to him. His front hall was a standing challenge of the Buffon Theory.

"I adhere to the Linnaean," Jefferson said once, when discussing the best way to classify animals. Insisting that Linnaeus offered nothing intrinsically better than other systems, Jefferson declared he would follow it "mainly because it has got into so general use that it will not be easy to displace it." The Linnaean naming project, ultimately global, had begun humbly in 1735. A Swedish nobleman who used the Latin pseudonym Linnaeus, produced an eleven-page pamphlet, *Systema Naturae*, and then revised and republished it in longer editions until it snowballed to become the world's standard taxonomic bible. The Linnaean Society of New England, the president of which was Judge John Davis, was the Boston branch of the international project of volunteers who wanted to do nothing less than catalogue all life on earth.

Even so, to Davis, Jefferson was not an ally nor a friendly competitor, but his nemesis.

It could not be otherwise. Davis's score was personal.

Davis was one of President Adams's Midnight Judges, Federal judges approved by a Federalist-heavy Senate not really at midnight but still only a few days ahead of Thomas Jefferson's inauguration. These judges were branded interlopers (when speakers were polite), and were heatedly condemned by Jeffersonians, drunk or sober, who claimed that the courts had been stolen by the Federalist Party, a charge that made Davis one of the thieves. Jefferson himself sharply claimed that these judges were put in place to cheat the American people out of the regime change for which the people had voted.

Federalists took offense.

Adams did not attend Jefferson's inauguration. Once close friends, Adams and Jefferson did not speak or write one another for over a decade. Upon resuming correspondence, Adams, still smoldering, soon brought up the judges. Jefferson deftly avoided discussion by suggesting that they let history judge the judges.

Davis was under no such obligation.

Davis—tenured for life in an office sometimes called "the last one-man fiefdom in Western civilization" and enshrined in a courtroom that put judges on a raised platform, above the bar to whom they are literally the law—in his most unpopular decision, upheld Jefferson's Embargo Act, a law that crippled New England economically. It was a law that the seaport boy on the Federal bench surely and personally thought unwise and no doubt a decision over which he may have brooded, hoping one day to even scores with Jefferson. The sea serpent, in Davis's hands, was a weapon of revenge. Not the bone collectors to the South, with Jefferson among them, but Judge Davis and his small team of Northerners (and Federalists) would load, take aim, fire and finally win the cultural war for the United States of America.

Whatever his motivation, Judge Davis sensed the arrival of his hour. He wanted a committee, testimony, depositions, signed statements, names, dates, times, places, colors, thicknesses, lengths, distances and materials for a broadside that would take the French scientists by storm; it would be a surprise to arrogant men whose books he had carefully read and copied out of at the Athenaeum. Driven by the idea of vicarious discovery through witnesses of Gloucester's squirming sea serpent, Judge Davis activated what appears to have been at best a relaxed Pickwickian gentlemen's club. From among members of his Boston chapter of the Linnaean Society of New England, Davis broke up the agenda of gentlemen who shared books, pooled their stuffed birds and sea shells into a collection kept in a room they rented at Boyle's Market and took part in social evenings on Saturdays, probably followed by cheese, crackers and sherry. The fifty-six-year-old Judge Davis sensibly recruited the help of two able, younger men, Dr. Jacob Bigelow and attorney Francis Gray.

Jacob Bigelow, MD, thirty years old and the bigger scientific gun of the two, was born in Waltham in 1787 and was largely a self-taught scholar. The Linnaean Society of New England was founded in his front parlor in 1814. Before becoming a Phi Beta Kappa graduate of Harvard, as a little boy he learned Latin on the sly after his father locked up the Latin books "for riper years." But the handy, athletic Bigelow also recalled having "wasted his time in roving about the woods," designing traps to catch rats and squirrels, drawing and carving, while taking "intense delight in the construction of miniature saw-mills." He took a medical degree from the University of Pennsylvania, where one of his teachers was Dr. Benjamin Rush, a signer of the Declaration of Independence and the author, in 1811, of the first American book on mental diseases. Bigelow's own first book was an 1814 catalogue of Boston flowers in Latin, *Florula bostoniensis*, which he illustrated himself. It was vouched for by Dr. Asa Gray as "a popular and satisfactory work" but ultimately obsolete as "the last manual of this and perhaps any other country arranged upon the Linnaean artificial system." A Swiss botanist who took note of the rising Linnaean star saw to it that over thirty species of *Bigelovia* were named after him. Bigelow, a popular Boston physician who lectured at the Harvard Medical School and held a professorship in applied science as well, wrote pamphlets on medical topics derived from his own experiences with patients. Without question, Linnaeus-loyal Bigelow served as the committee's chief scientific consultant and did the illustrations of its book. Newly married for only four months to Mary Scollay, Bigelow reported for duty to Judge Davis but the honeymooner shrewdly and simultaneously drafted more help by calling upon his bachelor friend, Francis Calley Gray, to be the team's workhorse, or amanuensis.

Bigelow, rather than Judge Davis, knew the gregarious Gray, who was twenty-seven years old and a man capable of being heard, possessing an operatic voice that could carry to the edge of a crowd and making him an in-demand public speaker. In 1815, Bigelow and Gray, with three others including Judge Lemuel Shaw (later Chief Justice Shaw and father-in-law of Herman Melville) and two native guides, climbed Monadnock in New Hampshire and Ascutney in Vermont. By Bigelow's account, the party scaled these mountains, searching for alpine plants, which was "an arduous undertaking, owing to the rough state of the country and the want of roads or paths." Atop Monadnock, beside a small fire on which a kettle for stew boiled, "it being the Fourth of July, Mr. Gray was invited to deliver an impromptu address."

After he came down from the mountain, Gray continued to speak. Two months after beginning the sea serpent study, in October 1817, Gray made a speech before the Massachusetts Charitable Financial Society; the next year, the city of Boston invited him to be its Fourth of July keynote speaker. A junior diplomat and world traveler recently back from serving Ambassador John Quincy Adams, Gray may have required coaxing from Bigelow or Judge Davis before his natural *bonhomie* kicked in. Gray had no innate interest in chasing sea serpents. His natural pursuits were in the fields of arts and letters, although he dabbled in amateur photography in the 1840s. William T. Davis, in his 1895 memoir of Boston lawyers and judges, did not highlight Gray's forensic gifts or famous cases. "His life was devoted chiefly to literary pursuits," Davis said succinctly of Gray. The author of books about colonial laws and penology, Gray also published pamphlets on education reform and poems, wrote for the *North American Review* magazine and collected and bequeathed a huge collection of rare European engravings to Harvard.

Gray's diary, now at Duke University library (and a "researcher's dream" of legibility), includes neat notes of his February 1815 trip to Monticello. Gray had supped with the devil—and liked him. Those entries were not published until 1924. Gray doubtless kept his visit to Jefferson a secret from his Federalist friends Davis and Bigelow.

Judge Davis reported with precision when his committee began its work on August 19, 1817, but not where the trio met. Possible locations are the doctor's office, a borrowed room of the Harvard Medical School, the judge's chambers or Gray's law office at Barrister's Hall. Judge Davis also did not specify whether a vote was taken or that a decision was made at a regular meeting of the society to form the committee. Quite possibly, the committee was organized pursuant to the emergency edict of Judge Davis, the society's president, who was acting alone.

Judge Davis, Dr. Bigelow and Attorney Gray, possessing varying degrees of excitement and varying personal and family responsibilities and interests, immediately decided to conduct the sea serpent project without leaving the

"Athens of America." Davis, married with five children, had long lived in Boston, where sessions of his court were held, while the honeymooner Bigelow lived on Summer Street and practiced out of an office on Tremont Street, and Gray had at least his art collection to consider. Expecting testimonial rather than real evidence and sightings rather than a specimen, they decided to deputize a deposition-drafter. Their agent on site in Gloucester, Justice of the Peace Lonson Nash, was a natural.

Gloucesterites, so far in back of the pack that they did not know they were in competition, were being invited to ride at the front of the worldwide parade of scientific progress. The seaport of Gloucester in the northeastern corner of Massachusetts, far from great experiments, was the small town where Andrew Robinson had designed and sailed the first schooner in 1713; it was a town not built on a rock but around a body of water, fairly made to be depicted by the Hudson River school of artists, in pastels with rainbows, sails and signs of lazy breezes, where the schooner remained its basic fishing vessel and haystacks moved on pole-pushed rafts along the Annisquam River. In 1817, around the town you could see skiffs, sailboats, rowboats of freckled boys and beribboned girls, seine boats out at dawn for mackerel, larger ships in full sail headed to South America with the tide and men and boys crouching in the many sail lofts of Gloucester, measuring, cutting and sewing canvas; you could hear the noise of the blacksmith's hammer against his anvil, the taps and curses of coopers making barrels and, at Somes's ropewalk by the Cut, men and boys painstakingly working fibers, thickening strands into rope; and you could smell the horsey odor of the streets blended with the effluvia of long racks of gutted, split codfish drying in the open air. The spirit of scientific discovery may have filled the American air generally, but it was lost in the drowsy air over this saltwater version of Hannibal, Missouri. The town's harbor skyline boasted two windmills not as a sign that the town was a hotbed of technological invention but as a reminder that old European technology was recycled. Before Judge Davis convened his little committee, there had been no likelihood that the town of fishermen, rich merchants, well-to-do captains and a few struggling farmers on the edge of the American continent, at the tip of Cape Ann, would play a historic role in the annals of American science. But, through Justice Nash, Gloucesterites who had never heard of the Linnaean project would soon learn that no Linnaean Society anywhere could expect to discover anything bigger, uncover anything more legendary or deal with any creature more exciting than the sea serpent that was visiting their harbor. Justice Nash would have explained to anyone who would stop scanning the horizon and listen a minute, all about the Buffon Theory, that North American animals were not as big as Old World animals or that its spectrum of species was not as wide as in Europe. If he invoked names, Nash would have argued that Gloucester could beat Jefferson at his own game, and that the Buffons of Europe and the Jeffersons of the South, in order to keep up with changing science, would have to buy the book that Gloucester put together.

The committee sent Nash a list of questions and detailed written instructions. Basically, the committee recycled litigation rules to ensure against a hoax.

Nash was to sequester the witnesses he selected; the witnesses were to give their answers individually, separately, outside of one another's hearing; and they could not discuss the sea serpent or their answers with one another until all of the depositions were completed and signed.

Nash could not cross examine. The committee prepared a list of twenty-five questions, a straightjacket Nash was to ask of every witness, no more and no less. There was one critical omission: there were no exclusionary questions. Witnesses themselves volunteered that what they saw was not a whale, a horse mackerel or any other sea creature they had seen; they said they were confident—that they knew these other types of animals. But the committee had risked getting back no comparisons. For a scientist, knowledgeable comparisons are the foundation from which to prove the "new" part of any claimed "new species." This point the committee assumed; all twenty-five of its questions asked for details about an assumed new species.

After Nash recorded the witness's answers, each witness was to review his statement (Nash selected only men) as a true and accurate record to which he would swear before signing in front of the justice, who would notarize the signature.

Then, Nash was to bundle up the packet of raw material and ship it to Judge Davis in Boston for the committee's ostensibly cool, temperate and objective review and analysis.

That was the plan.

Chapter 4

LONSON NASH, ALL FOR LOVE

If Nash had been a character in a play, the stage direction preceding his lines would read, "Enter, the Lover." Surely the most attractive character of the saga of Gloucester's sea serpent, Nash was a romantic lead stranded in a prosaic port. His chief claim to fame, as half of a great and lifelong romance, was written on water while his brief role serving as one summer's scribe of the sea serpent study is ironically preserved and still the source of quotes. This book aims to do Nash rough justice by recognizing, for the first time, both his lifelong and his summertime role. "Nabby" is the answer to questions like: Why didn't Nash live as a political lawyer in his childhood home, Great Barrington, where he first entered the practice of law? Why wasn't Nash in Boston, where he might have done better?

The task of reconstructing the course of true love is not easy. One is tempted to imagine a scene out of *Tom Jones*—sheer speculation but, nonetheless, if an inference is correct from the memorial of his Essex Bar colleagues after he died. In the memorial, his colleagues praised Nash as "a gentleman of the old school in his manners, life and principles"; so he was no slovenly rake but a snappy dresser when snappy dressing meant knickers, a tricorn hat, a ruffled shirt, a fine vest, a wine-red jacket and silver-buckle shoes. Presidents wore knickers through James Monroe's time. Accordingly, when Nash's presumed stagecoach stopped before Jonathan Lowe's tavern in 1806 or '07 or when he made his way to the tavern after getting off the boat in Gloucester harbor, the newly minted member of

If Lonson Nash came to Gloucester by ship, then he passed Eastern Point as he entered the harbor. Long before the breakwater was built, Eastern Point and the Old Fort across from it were like two outstretched arms embracing the harbor. In August 1817, Eastern Point was the backdrop of several sea serpent sightings. The earliest sea serpent sighting reported by Justice Nash was by Mariner Amos Story, who observed the sea serpent frolicking in waters between Ten Pound Island and Eastern Point. *Courtesy of Roseanne Cody.*

the Massachusetts bar—a native of western Massachusetts and a college boy—would have cut a figure that invited glances, if not awestruck stares, in provincial Gloucester.

Nash left no memoir of his love or love letters and poems to Nabby, nor do documents survive from Nabby Nash. While Venus and her Adonis, Troilus and his Cressida, Pyramus and his Thisby, Aeneas and his Dido, and o, sir and madam, star-cross'd Romeo and his ill-fated Juliet are all celebrated couples long lauded, sadly, the story of Lonson and Nabby Nash and how they lived on Western Avenue in Gloucester was never set to verse.

We can only grope toward a vague sense of Lonson Nash's early years. Official records reveal the bare fact that British-born Lonson Nash, when he was fifteen to seventeen years old, took the oath of citizenship before a judge in the courthouse in Pittsfield. Although it was surely a life-changing event, its context does not survive. This act may reflect a rebellious boy who became an American citizen over his loyalist father's objections, who promptly disinherited his son. Nash could have been a Revolutionary War orphan separated from his mother or father, or both; if they were Tories, taken up by another family. Or, after the revolution, as Tories took ships back to England or resettled in Canada, one could imagine a bold, even headstrong teenager refusing to go to Nova Scotia or back to England and rebelliously swearing in as an American citizen, casting his lot with the fragile, new republic. It could have been, at best, an action taken for love of his mother if she were American-born or his ally and co-conspirator in the transaction. However tumultuous his teen years may have been, Nash not only graduated from college but somehow apprenticed with an older attorney and began to practice law as a member of the Massachusetts bar.

What he accomplished in attending college, graduating and finding a position in law and sponsor to become admitted to the bar were all radically unusual achievements at that time—all the more so if the young man was a product of a dysfunctional family. Unusual again, Attorney Nash at the start of his law practice traveled from western Massachusetts. The journey from Great Barrington to Gloucester at the tip of Cape Ann, a long, bumpy trip either entirely on horseback or by stage, or partly on the rolling deck of a ship, was easily a journey, from start to finish, of a week to ten days. But, it seems circumstantially very probable, when he walked through the tavern door, she was waiting.

The love of his life had her home in Gloucester. Was it good luck that he found her while in the seaport for business? Or, by one obvious possibility, is it not likely that Nash had relatives in Gloucester? After all, among the early settlers of Great Barrington was a large Gloucestershire, England contingent; and, among those who settled the spit of land that Captain John Smith had dubbed Cape Tragibigzanda were those who renamed it Gloucester in honor of their own hometown in England. Is it impossible that one family from Gloucester, England, scattered its gene pool widely, both on Cape Ann and in the Berkshires? That speculation would naturally spawn the further possibility that Nash's Gloucester relatives found him a prospective wife, sent him a locket with her picture and snippets of her hair and encouraged him to court Nabby by correspondence—before he ever met her—and to set up a practice in a seaport with, his relatives would have assured him, good future prospects. His putative relatives may have arranged things to happen quickly.

Or Cupid simply drew his bow.

Her birth name was probably Abigail, but everybody called her "Nabby." Nabby was even the name on their marriage certificate, the formal Lonson was his, but we may imagine that she called him her dear Lonny. Nabby, the tavern keeper's daughter, possessed one of the first faces Nash saw in Gloucester. Eye contact, smiles and a meaningful glance or two set the two young erstwhile strangers in motion toward intimacy.

For homegrown Nabby, however the romance began, Nash would have been an exotic catch. They were opposites: Nabby was nestled in the bosom of her extended and close family, and Lonny was the stranger in town whose distant family may have ceased to function before he was in his teens. Before he ever walked through the threshold of Lowe's tavern, it is obvious that Lonson Nash had made a series of decisions of a kind Nabby never faced, and his maturity may have come across in a confident and radiant way.

Gloucester, no stranger to odd couples even in our time, on September 26, 1807, was the site of the wedding between Nash—a twenty-seven-year-old, Williams College graduate, naturalized American citizen and literate, witty and well-mannered Federalist—and Nabby—his presumably beautiful, presumably blushing and definitely disenfranchised bride (women did not vote) who was nineteen years old and a Gloucester born-and-raised daughter of the town's tavern keeper and stagecoach operator.

The likelihood is that Nash fell head over heels for his sweet Nabby, a love that explains why he made Gloucester his home. But it is also a fact that, through Nabby, Nash simultaneously established a family connection of great use to him as a rising Federalist. Jonathan Lowe—the operator of the stage between Gloucester and Boston, Nabby's doting father and whose son John would grow up to serve Gloucester as representative and senator—was also a tavern keeper during an era that tavern keepers held the keys to the State House. Newspapers aside, taverns were the news media of the time. Tavern owners literally published the news as people came and went. Who had better access to the public ear throughout a campaign than Jonathan Lowe?

As long as Jonathan Lowe lived, Lonson Nash, a stranger in these parts, enjoyed meteoric success politically. He ascended up the Federalist Party's ranks from mere supporter to speaker, representative, senator and delegate. The year after the Federalist supporter married Nabby, in 1808, he was the keynote speaker at the Gloucester Federalists' Fourth of July party; the following year, 1809, he was a freshman in the legislature as Gloucester's elected representative in the Great and General Court; and, in 1812, within a larger district beyond his Gloucester base, he was elected senator. At the Federalists' special "war and peace" convention in 1813, Nash was one of Gloucester's delegation of four. Nash was a mover and shaker and a

Federalist playing on the national stage with other idealists when the party's antiwar position became official.

During the war years, while Gloucester housewives suffered—years that Nabby would have found challenging—Nash would have been living the most dramatic and exciting years of his career. With the coming of peace in 1815 and as Federalism ended, Jonathan Lowe died. Nash could not or, at least, did not make a political comeback. After hobnobbing with exhilarated Federalist Party leaders during the most volatile times, Nash found himself a politician out of office and in the wrong party. Nash—not one of the merchants and captains who lived in the big houses around the harbor but surviving in their service—worked for the rest of his life to support Nabby and three sons and two daughters in Gloucester, the town Nabby apparently deeply loved.

(The number of Nash sons and daughters reflect an informed guess. Nabby and Lonny had a moderately large family for those days but, as any researcher of early American families knows, early census rosters list people in homes by various age groups under a named head of household. Supposed minor children may actually be domestic servants, apprentices, distant relatives, students or lodgers. Similarly, five children may be five decennial survivors. It is impossible to know if the Nashes had a dozen children and lost more than half of them to childhood diseases or accidents or had five and all five survived; one will never know how often a mourning wreath and black crepe went up on the door and over their lintel. There may have been more—or slightly fewer—children. At least two daughters and one son survived to adulthood.)

We draw the curtain on further speculation about Nash's decision to relocate in Gloucester. Curiously enough, Nash seems never to have forsaken the green hills of western Massachusetts. Perhaps Nash even returned periodically or seasonally to the west or produced a stream of chatty letters to keep his contacts fresh with school chums or friends or relatives. The surviving certain fact is that Great Barrington and the Berkshires exercised such a pull upon Nash that, when he was an old and ill man after Nabby had presumably died, he left Gloucester for Great Barrington when he retired in 1859 or 1860.

Any comparison between Judge Davis and Lonson Nash as lovers cannot be made and is immaterial. But another comparison is practical and relevant. While Judge Davis represented a sort of American Pickwick whose income was steady, whose gentlemanly status was assured, whose popularity was enduring, whose coterie of followers were lifelong loyal, a charismatic Judge who could run any group that wanted him and whom all of the learned groups headquartered in Boston wanted to lead them, Lonson Nash, poor but honest, lived with his one true, loyal love, Nabby, and his children, earning a slim living handling some of the few cases filed and heard or settled for consideration acknowledged by and between the town's merchant-litigants and shipmaster-litigants, their heirs and assigns. Nash never seemed to have had the great good fortune to become embroiled in one of Gloucester's wonderful, interminable, lawyer-devouring religious controversies over who owns the communion silver after a congregation divides or Gloucester cases that made their way to the supreme judicial court, but he at least made enough to survive.

Accordingly, to the Nash house, Judge Davis's request would have clearly been an imposition. Nabby may have wondered, privately, how her husband would spare the time to accomplish depositions. However, it is obvious from the cheerful replies Nash sent and his extensive cooperation that he was himself exceedingly pleased and even grateful. After all, in contrast to his usual routine in Gloucester, which Nash already interrupted to see the sea serpent, Judge Davis's summons broke through dark clouds. Nash, in his houseful of kids, amid probable genteel poverty and with few paying clients needing his services, was smilingly game to serve Judge Davis. When the judge's surprising summons came, Nash welcomed it as a way to oblige the gentleman who was a Federalist model if not a mentor to him. For Nash, the sea serpent project constituted a last hurrah and a splendid revival of polished contacts from his happiest days.

The calendar is evidence of Nash's immediate and positive response. Judge Davis issued the committee's invitation on August 19 and Nash, probably receiving it on August 20, sat with his first witness, Solomon Allen III, on August 21. Why did he jump with such alacrity? Certainly, he scrambled in part because nobody knew how much longer the sea serpent would be in town. But also, he wanted to please and impress Judge Davis. Nash skirted obstacles and avoided delay by recruiting deponents from among people of his own circle. Possibly clients, certainly merchants, shipowners and skilled tradesmen were his easy targets. Nash's deponents were primarily men of business, folks responsible for making accurate records themselves and organized and efficient people who hustled along the waterfront for whom speaking on the record would be no problem.

Nash also finally reduced the time required to generate reports by interviewing only a representative sample, although this may have been by default rather than by design. In his letters to Judge Davis, Nash mentioned witnesses he talked to who gave him no signed statements; whether those people turned him down or if Nash simply decided not to depose them is not clear.

In the end, even after including his own unsworn statement, Nash offered Judge Davis only nine out of over a hundred potential witnesses. That was all to Judge Davis, whom Nash wanted to please and impress. If greater Gloucester cooperation was sought, it was denied. A tacit, superstition-based boycott of the scientific study of the sea serpent may have existed almost townwide. Gloucester's C.L. Sargent later only found sixteen witnesses, some of whom seemed to have been only grudgingly cooperative, and he had points to recommend him to Gloucester's seafaring community.

Stephanie Buck, the Cape Ann Museum's archivist and librarian, found that Gloucester's native enthusiast of the sea serpent, C.L. Sargent (born in Gloucester in 1778), was forty when the sea serpent appeared. Charles Lenox Sargent, a sea captain in the East India service and the son of Epes Sargent Jr. and Dorcas (Babson) Sargent, may never have seen the sea serpent. Possibly in poor health by then—he died in January 1820—in the three or four years before he died, too young to retire, the sea captain was curiously devoted to writing. Married as he was to Mary Turner, formerly of Duxbury, I imagine him as a responsible provider, working feverishly and racing against time and his mortality, in order that his widow would not suffer want. These were days before Social Security. Probably not for his own amusement, then, but for his widow-to-be, he published two books in quick succession, a technical manual in 1817 called *A System of General Signs for Night and Day*, and a semi-autobiographical novel, *Alexander Smith, Captain of the Island of Pitcairn*, in 1819. Sargent ran out of time, but before he died, he filled half of a notebook with the sea serpent sightings that he transparently hoped to publish as a third book, one about Gloucester's sea serpent of 1817.

His notes reflect an oddly limited access to the people he interviewed. Some obstacle seems to have precluded lengthy discussion. It was as if Sargent only briefly, in passing, could grab the occasional attention of people passing by his home or sickbed. His notes, varying little in their length, are all quick sketches of individual sightings. Some people apparently departed too hastily for him to note their full names, "Wife of Trask" and "Mrs. Moore" among them, people who may not have given Sargent their full names, or whom he (or another informant of his) overheard or he received secondhand.

Among the witnesses missed by Nash and C.L. Sargent were the first of Gloucester's sea-serpent sighters.

Chapter 5
THE LEGENDARY LADIES

August 6

Two unnamed women, whose stories were supposedly dismissed as old wives' tales, reputedly first saw the Gloucester sea serpent of 1817. Their stories appeared in some magazines, newspapers and much more recent books and not in Judge Davis's or C.L. Sargent's collections.

Bernard Heuvelmans, in *In the Wake of the Sea-Serpents*, wrote with geographical circumlocution, "On 6 August 1817 two women saw a sea-monster like a huge serpent come into the harbour of Cape Ann which lies north of Gloucester roads." Like Heuvelmans, who said that little attention was paid to their report until several fishermen confirmed the news, J.P. O'Neill, in *The Great New England Sea Serpent*, wrote what he called "an oft told tale" of two women and a coaster "reported seeing something strange in the water" on August 6, but no one believed them. Indeed, he said that the coaster, who spoke about a sixty-foot sea serpent at "the entrance to the bay," was supposedly "driven out of Lipple's auction room with derogatory laughter."

The legend has its plausible aspects.

For one thing, Gloucesterites then, especially women, got about town on foot, often in pairs (a wise precaution, as they quoted the Bible for its saying, "If one stumbles, the other may help"), not on paved two-lane roads but over paths between trees and brush that snaked through the woods and ran narrowly along the sides of hills. Only the broadest and most-often used roads in Gloucester—trade roads, really—were cleared for the use of carts, carriages and horses. The hypothetical ladies would have consequently made slow progress and they would have paused occasionally during their journey, especially if August 6 was a hot and humid day. Although no document survives to tell whether the women were running an errand together, fetching water or visiting a sick friend, we really need none. Helping neighbors in need, local women were Gloucester's nurses and midwives. Before telephones or Meals on Wheels, the assistance available to the sick, the mothers in labor and the elderly were female neighbors.

Whether they were Gloucester women running charitable errands or well-to-do ladies on a hardy recreational walk on the fragile and spidery circuit of dusty dirt roads and paths in early August, the pair walked, talked and passed alongside the harbor, catching a breath of salt air as they proceeded along rutted and rocky roads that scarcely deserved the name. One scanned the harbor, hoping to pick out familiar boats coming in and, if so, to gauge how heavy-laden or fish-rich the vessel appeared to be. Lean years made for sharp eyes. At a glance, locals could literally judge whether any particular neighbor's ship had come in.

The woman who saw it first—something that cut through the glassy surface of the harbor below and beside them, leaving a long wake—would have called out to the other, no doubt pointing, until they were both looking, probably shielding their eyes with their hands to see better the elongated animal that moved in eerie silence as it swam swiftly by them and entered the harbor.

What on earth was it?

Neither would have ever seen anything like it.

When they returned home, among their day's adventures was a story to share about the flash of a great fish perhaps, although very long. Whether their husbands or children reacted with interest or disbelief is nowhere reported but their story may have gone further as a rumor. Given the level of education offered to women at that time, neither took pen in hand to write her account or to dictate it and mark "X" for their signature. In any case, there was no newspaper in Gloucester to notify or radio or television stations to run the women's story. It is safe to say that, had the sea serpent not stayed in the warm basin of broad Gloucester harbor thereafter, creating a period that led to sightings by many others—including men prominent locally—the old wives' tale of what the women saw would have been utterly lost to history.

The world without records that the adult men and women of 1817 had been born into was on the verge of changing. It was too late for two illiterate women but, once the sea serpent was spotted by men, the world of literate men and regular records lurched into gear. The sea serpent's frolics before a wider audience, including Judge Davis, had begun.

One wonders whether the legendary ladies are composites of informants who spoke with C.L. Sargent.

Although none of the reports gathered by C.L. Sargent is of two women on August 6, among the vignettes stored at the Cape Ann Museum is the account of Susan Stover, who, "about the 10th August, 1817" in the company of her father "near the shore by the house" saw the sea serpent, whom she described as having a head "very plain of the shape of a dog" so near the shore that "her father took off his hat that he should not frighten him." (Obviously, he was wearing his sea-serpent-scaring hat!) Hats off quite rightly to the sea serpent—he did his best trick, a full circle. Ms. Stover "saw him turn in the water and the parts pop in opposite direction." Between bones and cartilage, the sea serpent's flexibility to maneuver strongly suggests cartilage.

C.L. Sargent also found another woman, Lydia Wonson, who, supposedly on August 10, "standing in the house" where she lived on Eastern Point, looked out "between the house and Ten Pound Island" to see something in the harbor not more than a quarter-mile away. It "looked like the buoys of a seine," was sixty or seventy feet on the surface of the water and with a spyglass, she saw the creature "draw himself up into a coil and extend himself again." For nearly a half hour, Ms. Wonson kept him "fairly and plainly in view, his head out of water about as large as a horse's head." Also on August 10, a Sunday, in "the cove that makes up the isthmus of Rocky Neck" and coming to "within a stone's throw" of him, William Row saw "the serpent and two sharks come into the cove." Row said that his sons dispatched one of the sharks at some point that he did not identify. The sea serpent "frequently put his head out of water as if to swallow his game," Row told Sargent, judging that the trio followed schools of baitfish. He moved "rapidly" but not so fast that Row could not make out a head that was cryptically "as broad as a horse's and more so or not quite so long." Row insisted that, all told, having seen the sea serpent several times, including August 14, he "could not be deceived about him."

The sighting dated "about the 10th August" by Susan Stover may have been earlier than the sighting made on August 10 by Amos Story, Lonson Nash's earliest sea-serpent sighter. Susan Stover and Lydia Wonson in some garbled mix-up may account for the legendary ladies of August 6 who populate some published accounts.

Unlike the legend, by the way, the first sighters may have been believed. Gloucester people were probably not as astonished to see a sea serpent as we may imagine. The reports of their initial incredulousness, local ridicule and laughing someone out of the tavern may be exaggerated or made up out of whole cloth. After storms, Gloucester people have always found strange remains washed ashore and, doubtless, would have heard tales as John Josselyn had. Along the Massachusetts coast, the clear sighting of a sea serpent off Plymouth had been a common rumor only a couple of years earlier. Besides mundane sources, from preachers and from reading the Bible, they knew of leviathans of the deep.

In the Bible, sea serpents were identified with God's punishment; the sea serpent's death was Israel's deliverance.

"In that day the Lord with his sore and great and strong sword shall punish leviathan," the King James version said in Isaiah 27:1, "the piercing servant, even leviathan, that crooked serpent; and he shall slay the dragon that is in the sea."

When he was not parting the Red Sea for his people, biblical authors saw that the Lord "brakest the heads of the dragons in the waters," splitting their heads to pieces (Psalms 74: 13–14). The sea serpent was literally cooked when the time arrived that the Lord was well disposed to the chosen people.

"There go the ships: there is that leviathan, whom thou hast made to play therein," read Psalms 104:26, until the Lord gave it to his people for "meat in due season." The creatures of the deep sea were beyond human power.

God asked Job with a mocking tone in Job 41:1, "Canst thou draw out leviathan with a hook? or his tongue with a cord which thou lettest down?" to which the answer is obviously negative. But, as an eerie stand-in, the sea serpent is presented as a proxy for divine power. "None is so fierce that dare to stir him up: who then is able to stand before me?" Job 41:10.

Bible-reading, pious folks who observed the sea serpent under the influence of Isaiah, the Psalmists and Job would have understood that they were being sent a warning by prodigy. Such beliefs, equating freaks of nature with divine decrees, are traditional. "Monster" is, in fact, the English version of the Latin *monstrum*, the word for omen. No one wanted to tangle with the strange, silent animal in the harbor. Mostly grizzled veterans of life on the sea, or hard-headed men of business, the men who reported their sightings to their local Justice Nash—except for brave Gaffney, who was armed, and nervous John Johnston Jr., who was a teenager—noted the sea serpent's characteristics at a respectful distance, football fields away.

The people of Gloucester would have possessed the mainstream belief that God had created sea monsters. The Bible said so. It followed that whatever God created still existed. How often the beasts from the bottom of the sea would appear was a matter of God's plan.

Jefferson, who read his Bible scientifically, cutting and pasting the parts he felt could be sworn to in a court of law, entertained a similar premise. One day when he wondered whether animals, once created, could ever become extinct, he flipped through his books to substantiate his hypothesis. Fresh after his directed reading, Jefferson (as a representative of the best-educated, most well-traveled and scientifically inclined Americans of his generation) wrote, "Such is the economy of nature that no instance can be produced of her having permitted any one race of her animals to become extinct." This thinking is what made him so sure that any link in the chain of life, once formed, had never broken. Accordingly, it is why Jefferson not only sent Lewis and Clark to explore the new Louisiana Purchase lands but also told them to keep an eye out for mammoths.

Judge Davis, a Bible reader and note taker who followed Linnaeus, in 1817 visualized the leviathan of the Lord—created and never destroyed, on the loose and ready to be named. Jefferson's mammoth was Judge Davis's leviathan, Jefferson's Lewis and Clark team was Judge Davis's Lonson Nash. Judge Davis set Justice Nash in motion to get sightings of the sea serpent down on paper. The earliest sighting Nash was able to preserve was that of a Gloucester mariner, Amos Story.

Chapter 6
STORY'S SIGHTING

August 10

Amos Story said that he was a mariner—a respectful term broad enough to touch the rank of a navigator or a boatswain, while still, with only a dash of euphemism, covering a fisherman or a crew member. Through mariner Amos Story's eyes, one sees not only the sea serpent but also, between the lines of his report, the largely self-set pace of activities of a mariner on his day of rest for, on Sunday, August 10, Amos Story did not need to stop doing anything, to put down the net he was mending, to leave off stocking a schooner or setting sail for Georges Banks. At noon on the Sabbath, in the rhythm of life in the town of Gloucester in 1817, Story did not need to explain or to excuse the one-and-a-half hour period he spent staring at the surface of the outer harbor, where a creature was splashing.

"I was setting on the shore," Story said, his pronunciation of "setting" for "sitting" neatly caught in the transcription by Nash. When he estimated that he was "about twenty rods from him [the sea serpent] when he was the nearest to me," Story was emphasizing how good a look he got and how close the serpent came. Twenty rods is just over a hundred yards. Story and the serpent were never closer than about a football field away from one another.

In broad daylight, beginning between high noon and 1 o'clock (Story obviously had no watch in his pocket) and at varying distances as the serpent moved toward and away, Story kept it in his sight for about an hour and a half. Story watched as the serpent cruised the waters south and east of Ten Pound Island. Essentially, to anybody looking at Ten Pound Island from

Ten Pound Island, pictured here as it is today, has a small lighthouse that it did not have in 1817. For obvious reasons, no sightings were made after the sun set. *Courtesy of Manuel Simoes.*

today's Stacy Boulevard, the sea serpent was in "back" of the island they see. The serpent was swimming in the area at the mouth of the harbor, on the seaward side of the largest of the two islands then in Gloucester harbor. (The other island, once known as Five Pound Island, is buried under today's Jodrey State Fish Pier.)

The serpent's speed struck him as most remarkable, and Story emphasized the fact.

"He moved very rapidly through the water," Story told Nash. "I should say a mile in two, or at most, in three minutes."

Fast? The serpent Story described was the cheetah of the sea. Although it was not a speedboat in full throttle, judged in today's terms, Story, an experienced man of the sea, was saying that he had seen the fastest thing on saltwater in 1817.

Unlike some other witnesses during later sightings, Story saw no "bunches on his back." Probably aware of this discrepant observation when he testified on August 23, Story further noted that he "did not see more than ten or twelve feet of his body." These observations were especially pertinent by August 23. With Gloucester's grapevine abuzz before August 23 about "rings and bunches," a phrase that Story likely heard, Story was sure that he had seen no "bunches," but he was also sure that he had seen no more than ten or twelve feet of "the serpent" at any time.

In another particular, Story was very fortunate. He got one of the best and longest looks ever of a sea serpent's head. The fast-moving animal's head was constantly in view for over an hour. It was something Story judged to resemble the head of a sea turtle.

"His head appeared shaped much like the head of the sea turtle, and he carried his head from ten to twelve inches above the surface of the water," Story recalled. But that was not the end of his comparisons. "His head at that distance appeared larger than the head of any dog that I ever saw. From the back of his head to the next part of him that was visible, I should judge to be three or four feet."

Without doubt, before Nash heard it, what Story saw on that Sunday had made the rounds in Gloucester, and people began to keep an eye out for the creature. Within a couple of days, a shipmaster, or sea captain, Solomon Allen III, joined the mariner's and the legendary ladies' club when he, too, saw the creature.

Chapter 7
ALLEN'S FIRST SIGHTING

August 12

Before going further, the conditions of Lonson Nash's project in Gloucester ought to be described or reconstructed for the reader. The steel-point nib, invented and manufactured in London since 1802, was not yet common in the United States. People still wrote with quill pens. They stopped to cut and split the featherweight goose-quill writing instrument with their "pen-knives." Fine quill pens were valued long after 1817. When Oliver Wendell Holmes Jr. took his place on the supreme judicial court in the 1890s, he found some quill pens in his desk. A court officer told him that they had been left behind by Chief Justice Shaw in the 1850s. It would be more than a decade before ex-Brit Richard Esterbrook organized a handful of craftsmen in Camden, New Jersey, to make metal pen nibs. Camden (coincidentally, in 1817, an unorganized part of Gloucester County, New Jersey) would also innovate by opening the country's first drive-in movie theater in 1933. But in 1817, there were no steel-point nibs or drive-ins even in Camden, and James Monroe wore knee britches, although he would be the last president to do so, at least publicly.

Putting our quill pen aside, in 1817, although writing could be done by candlelight or near a fire, writing was most typically done in daytime, using sunlight for illumination. Without electricity, computers or typewriters, the stenographers of the day took down summaries. Only partial verbatim transcripts exist. The Salem witch trials, for example, produced volumes that may still be inspected at the Massachusetts Archives at Columbia Point but there was no tradition that Nash would take down every exact word with his quill pen. He would always err on the side of the concise. He would certainly repeat back to the witness the answer, especially if shortened, for the witness to adopt or reject. After all, the witness was still to take an oath and sign the statement as accurate.

Nash, as a justice of the peace in Essex County, had likely equipped himself years earlier with a box-like wooden kit of quill pens, paper, ink and a writing board. Made to be compact and to fit on a sleigh or carriage, such a travel kit—the laptop of the time—had accompanied Thomas Jefferson to Philadelphia when he drafted the Declaration of Independence, and a similar kit had gone to war with George Washington as he dictated orders in the field to his secretary, Tobias Lear. Nash could never depend on the likelihood that a farmer or fisherman would have ink and pen or even paper. Many Gloucester homes and even some businesses had neither. Doubtless, Nash carried with him all of the stuff needed with which to record statements.

It is impossible to be certain today exactly where Nash set up his deposition factory. Of course, he may have written depositions at multiple sites. Itinerancy would have supported sequestration better than having witnesses take a number and line up at one central location. Possibly ignoring his own comfort and convenience, Nash had to bear in mind the committee's orders. He was under orders to insulate what he heard from the ears of a gossiping community. But he was also pressed to get the things out fast, and some days he took several depositions. A home office suggests itself but there may have been no such thing or, in 1817, as his house filled up with howling infants, his home office may have become the nursery, cradle and all. But Nash's witnesses would not have testified in the center of a crowded courtroom, and it is unlikely that a courtroom was used, with these particular depositions being, uniquely, no part of any judicial process. Besides, any roomy site used by judges in Gloucester in 1817, or by Nash as justice of the peace, was probably where the town meeting also met, and it would have been unnecessarily large. The deposition space only had to be well-illuminated and quiet. A cooperative tavern keeper might have set up a table and two chairs beside a second-floor window, a window blessedly open for breezes if the day were hot. Or someone may have offered the use of a room in their mansion, perhaps even a widow's walk. The room otherwise used for fish auctions, centrally located and well-known by all witnesses, may have been available. Certainly near the harbor, it is not impossible that Captain Elias Davis's home, today's Cape Ann Museum, which commemorates and displays sea serpent memorabilia, was the site of one or more depositions.

This D.G. Beers Gloucester harbor map (1872) shows several sites mentioned by deponents to Lonson Nash and C.L. Sargent and by crew members of the *Laura* to Judge Davis and his committee. For example, clockwise, note Norman's Woe, Webber's Cove ("Fresh Water Cove" on Beers's map), Piper's Rocks ("Field Rocks" on map), Stage Head, the Cut, the ubiquitous Ten Pound Island, Inner Harbor, Rocky Neck, Brace's Cove and Eastern Point. *Courtesy of the Cape Ann Museum.*

Nash's work would not have been performed very far from the Davis mansion, in any case.

Aware of the importance of gathering evidence when memories were fresh and comparatively independent of anyone else's recollections, within three days of the Davis committee's original formation on August 18, Nash conducted his first deposition, this one being Solomon Allen III, on August 21. To meet with witnesses one by one, alone, Nash arranged a staggered schedule. The eight witnesses testified on five different days.

Captain Solomon Allen, the first to speak with Nash, would have clomped over the wooden floor of whatever building Nash used, unless he treaded over a domestically felicitous rug.

Was Captain Allen cleanshaven or did he sport some sort of facial hair? About half of the male population seemed to wear beards, a European fashion that was spreading globally. Some gentlemen still used their razors at home over a basin of water that required a blazing fire if hot water were desired. Other gentlemen visited a barber, likely part time, who was available on certain days or certain hours each day. Barbers were also part-time surgeons licensed to "bleed" people. Doctors prescribed bleeding to eliminate the "bad blood" that caused a person's illness. According to theory, the body would then presumably kick in and make good blood to replace the loss. In 1799, George Washington was so bled that some historians think that he died by exsanguination. To this day, a red-and-white striped barber pole advertises barbers in mimicry of their bloodied white towels. Did Captain Allen have his own individual shaving mug at the barber's? Whether he shaved, was shaved or trimmed, he or his barber kept their razor sharp by vigorous use of a strop. It was 1817, when most everything— even a shave—was still handmade and individually tailored. But let us leave off speculating to conclude that Captain Allen came to Nash's presence with his recognizable, usual face.

Captain Allen or Nash would have certainly closed the door behind him and taken a seat opposite Nash. Then Nash, quill pen and bottle of ink at the ready, would have made a few remarks to put Allen at ease in general but also to remind him that he was speaking for the record, and that what he said he would be asked to swear to and to sign. After the preliminaries were spoken aloud, confirmed to have been understood and mutually agreed, Nash would have then told Allen to tell him about what he saw. As Allen told Nash that he was in a boat when he saw the serpent on the twelfth, Nash, with his head bowed over his paper, would have begun, carefully dipping his quill tip into ink and, with a practiced flourish, scratched words, letter by letter, until he filled the paper up with the first of Gloucester's sea serpent sightings to be captured on paper.

In amazing words today but common speech in Gloucester at the time, Allen told Nash, "I saw a strange marine animal, that I believe to be a serpent."

Certainly, Nash's witnesses' common denominator was that they had seen a strange marine animal that they believed to be a serpent and Nash knew a good thing when he heard it. Nash so introduced each deposition, recycling Allen's tag line. Invoking his words over and over, Justice of the Peace Nash proclaimed his fidelity again and again to Judge Davis's charge, assuring the committee that it was getting what they had asked for from his hand. Each time a witness came before Nash, he fit the same bill: he had seen a strange marine animal that he believed to be a serpent.

It is immediately notable that Allen called the sea serpent not "it" but "he." This was a custom followed by all of Nash's witnesses, as well as C.L. Sargent's informants. The custom will be followed in this book, although the sea serpent's gender can hardly have been known from the observations made in Gloucester. (The masculine pronoun seems to derive from the sheer size of the beast.) As to the serpent's size, Nash's first witness wanted it understood that he was in a position to give a good estimate. Allen told Nash that the sea serpent "was around him several times, within one hundred and fifty yards."

Unlike cautious Story later, Allen on the twenty-first told Nash that he was certain that the sea serpent was enormously long.

"I should judge him to be between eighty and ninety feet in length, and about the size of a half barrel, apparently having joints from his head to his tail," Captain Allen told Nash. From this, the Davis committee would have understood that Captain Allen was saying that he saw a "jointed" vertebrate, one capable of upward and downward slithering forward motion. Such locomotion would support those who said that the serpent was exceptionally fast, but Captain Allen on the twelfth saw the sea serpent at its most relaxed, manifestly enjoying a regular summer vacation day in August in Gloucester harbor.

"When he moved on the surface," Captain Allen described, "his motion was slow, sometimes playing about in circles, and sometimes nearly straight forward."

Captain Allen departed from Amos Story's later description by referring to the creature's dives.

"When he disappeared, he sunk apparently directly down," Captain Allen said, "and would next appear at two hundred yards from where he disappeared, in two minutes."

For its work, the committee had to determine whether the creature was air-breathing like a whale or it respired through gills like a shark. Captain Allen, present for more than an hour while the serpent kept its head about a foot above the waves and never seemed to dive, was hardly contradictory of the sea serpent being an air-breathing creature. Occasional dives lasting only a couple of minutes, behavior consistent again with an air breather, although it could hold its breath for a while underwater, were further observations that the committee would have been thrilled to read when they got to Allen's statements.

Captain Allen also had an unusually good view and recollection of the head of the animal as it "played about in circles" before him.

"His head formed something like the head of a rattle snake, but nearly as large as the head of a horse," he told Nash. He added that its color was a dark brown and, at least at the distance from which he observed it, the creature had no "spots upon him."

Nash probably hoped that when he asked if that was all, the gratifying witness had more. He did; he had seen the sea serpent another time, too, on August 13.

Chapter 8
ALLEN'S SECOND SIGHTING

August 13

Apparently Captain Allen took Wednesday off to look for the sea serpent. It paid off; although the sea serpent remained at a distance, Allen's view on August 13 was straight and unobstructed.

"I saw him nearly all day, from the shore," he told Nash. "I was on the beach, nearly on a level with him, and most of the time he was from one hundred fifty to three hundred yards from me."

By this point, we may imagine that Nash was following Allen word for word, not moving much in his chair, and probably on the edge of it, aware that Allen might well be not only his best witness by memory and articulation but one who had made multiple sightings that nobody else had. If Nash sensed anything, it was that speaking before him was the one man who had spent more hours in the presence of a sea serpent than anybody else on earth.

"Its joints or bunches, appeared about eight or ten inches above the surface of the water," Allen told his obviously engrossed scribe.

But then, in terms of locomotion, Captain Allen made a quite startling statement.

Justice Nash asked, "Did it bend its body up and down in moving, or to the right and left?"

Apparently with no hesitation, Allen answered, "He moved to the right and left."

With that response, Captain Allen suddenly ruined his credibility with Nash.

Coming along a few years after the sea serpent, this historic marine paint factory exemplifies Gloucester's "working harbor." Many of those who saw the sea serpent did so by stopping their work for a sea serpent break. *Courtesy of the Cape Ann Museum.*

As if that one answer were not bad enough, Allen followed with another answer immediately that Nash, from his own observations on August 14, also thought wrong.

When Nash asked him how many distinct portions of the serpent were out of water at one time, Allen said, "I should say fifty distinct portions."

Whether Nash put down his pen and stared at Allen at that moment or not, a week later when Nash picked up his pen and wrote to the Davis committee on August 28, Nash was brusque in his critique of what had at first seemed to be his best witness. He worried that the committee might accept Allen's major observations.

Unwilling to allow the Allen deposition to speak for itself, Nash told the committee flatly, "I am confident, from my own observation, that Mr. Allen is mistaken, as to the motion of the animal." Nash had seen, with his own eyes with the assistance of a telescope, the sea serpent in Gloucester harbor. In the cover letter he sent along with the packet of depositions, Nash declared to the committee that "his motion is vertical."

Nash added, still going by his own eyes, that Mr. Allen was "likewise mistaken, as to the distinct portions of the animal that were visible, at one time. I saw, at no time, more than eight distinct portions; though more may have been visible."

Having viewed the sea serpent twice through his glass, although he could not take in the whole serpent in one view, "and at other times, with the naked eye," Nash wanted the committee to know that he could not believe that fifty distinct portions were seen at any one time. Not only an eyewitness but the transcriber of depositions of seven other Gloucester witnesses besides Captain Allen, Nash went out further on a limb and said, "I believe the animal to be straight, and the apparent bunches were caused by his vertical motion."

Even so, no matter his good faith, given its limited foundation, Nash's one-line comment could not settle the dilemma that faced the committee: whether the sea serpent's vertical locomotion raised the illusion of several bunches on the water's surface, or whether the sea serpent's back was simply serially bumpy.

Curiously, although he strove hard to alert the committee against accepting the theory of a bumpy-backed sea serpent, little did Nash know how important that point would ultimately be or just how far into error that theory would take the committee members when, much later, it was presented with a bumpy-backed small land snake by none other than their same obedient servant, Lonson Nash.

Chapter 9

THE BIG SHOW

August 14

Augus 14, 1817, is the day that broke all prior records. It still stands as the greatest day of sea serpent sightings on earth and the one in which the sea serpent was supposed to die. Six of the nine Davis committee witnesses and eleven of the sixteen people C.L. Sargent interviewed saw the sea serpent on August 14.

Before all the excitement, Mary Row saw the sea serpent "early in the morning of August 14th" from her house between Rocky Neck and Ten Pound Island, the inner harbor. According to C.L. Sargent's notes, Miss Row, apparently at her window, saw the creature "in rapid motion and turned suddenly, his head going one way and his tail the other. Saw his head out of water very plain, seemed about as large as a horse, feels sure she saw 100 feet plainly on the surface of the water, saw him at different times after and had the same appearance."

Later, as C.L. Sargent also reported, a "Mrs. Moore" was "crossing the Cut" (today's Blynman Bridge) "without any previous knowledge of there being a serpent in our waters." That changed. When Mrs. Moore saw the creature "close to Piper's Rocks," she grew so alarmed that she "trembled like a leaf and stood some time in agitation." Her agitation ended because the sea serpent swam in the other direction. Mrs. Moore told Sargent that he "was very near and could not have been less than 100 feet plainly visible, saw him turn & move off in quick motion."

Captain Solomon Allen, who got his third, final and disappointing view of the sea serpent on the same day, told Justice Nash of August 14, "I saw him but once and had not so good a view of him."

Early on August 14, 1817, hours before Matthew Gaffney took a shot at the sea serpent, Mary Row viewed the creature from her home as "he" (all Gloucester witnesses used the masculine pronoun for the creature) swam swiftly from Rocky Neck toward Ten Pound Island. *Courtesy of Roseanne Cody.*

Mary Row, in a house that originally stood to the left of today's marine paint factory, visible here on the left, spectacularly saw the sea serpent "in rapid motion" turn suddenly, with "his head going one way and his tail the other." Ten Pound Island is ahead on the right, with the water in front of the island being, while Mary Row watched, the sea serpent's playground. *Courtesy of Manuel Simoes.*

Many others made an effort to get a good view and brought their spyglasses, as if they expected or hoped for a special event after the sea serpent had already been seen once or even several times by most of the witnesses deposed by Nash and who spoke with C.L. Sargent. Besides Allen, among the Davis committee's witnesses who looked at the harbor on August 14 from ship or from shore were Epes Ellery, shipmaster; William H. Foster, merchant; Lonson Nash; and Matthew Gaffney, ordinarily a ship carpenter, but that day the designated sea serpent executioner.

Epes Ellery, a descendant of one of Gloucester's oldest and most respected families (remember the White–Ellery house?), would not lightly take a false position or risk his family's humiliation by taking part in a hoax or being careless about his own observations. He answered Nash's questions on August 25.

Taking his turn in speaking with Justice Nash, Captain Ellery, about seventy years old, likely the oldest of the witnesses who testified, possibly with the grey beard that was then fashionable, a weather-beaten face but good, sharp eyes, demonstrated that he was an old salt. He measured his words, being notably conservative in his statements, and felt entirely free to tell Nash when he did not know anything. The old man of the sea was not only perfectly at home in using a spyglass or telescope—a skill that Nash envied and deemed himself defective in—he spoke comfortably about distances by "fathom" and made easy analogies to maritime items like two-gallon kegs.

Ellery seemed, nonetheless, to have arrived on August 14 after all of the excitement. At least, that was when he saw the sea serpent, at twilight time, "a little after the sun set" while he stood "on an eminence near low water mark" about thirty feet above sea level. With no indication of how long he had been standing there without seeing anything unusual, once the sun set and it was nearly time to leave and start for home, the old man suddenly saw something stir in the water. He judged the creature to be "about one hundred and fifty fathoms" from him. A fathom being six feet, Ellery was estimating that he saw it at a distance of some three hundred yards. It was quite a distance but Ellery claimed a clear view through his spyglass.

"I saw the upper part of his head, and I should say about forty feet of the animal," Ellery said, continuing to estimate that it appeared to him "to have joints, about the size of a two-gallon keg."

Ellery, in his focused way, did not say how many people he saw standing around the harbor or where the boats were. But he did add detail as background when he got more up to speed, and it became clear that there were still a lot of people and boats around the sea serpent, although Ellery limited himself to stating that there "were fifteen or twenty persons, near where I was." Quite possibly standing amid an excited crowd of people who were straining to see with or without spyglasses, Ellery was the one who hit the jackpot. Nobody had seen the creature open its mouth but he testified that on August 14, that day of so many sightings, he saw something nobody else had seen. Perhaps aware that his view was unique, he reported it very cautiously and precisely. "I was looking at him with a spy-glass," he said, "when I saw him open his mouth, and his mouth appeared like that of a serpent; the top of his head appeared flat."

Ellery's innate caution came through again when he described the serpent in motion. He told Nash that "when he turned it was quick, but I will not express an opinion of his velocity."

Thinking further on what he had seen, and contrary to his prior caution, he ventured a few words more on the subject:

"The first part of the curve that he made in turning was of the form of a staple, and as he approached toward his tail, he came near his body with his head, and then ran parallel with his tail, and his head and tail then appeared near together."

It is noteworthy that Nash, with his own spyglass that day and who had criticized Captain Allen about his August 10 report, wrote no contradiction of Ellery's remarks.

Asked about "bunches," as everyone was, cautious Ellery told Nash, "I did not count the number of bunches, but they appeared about six inches above the surface of the water."

Unlike Allen, Ellery said that the serpent's "sinuosities" were vertical.

Ellery described no timid sea serpent but a party animal. Delightfully phrasing what he saw, Ellery told Nash that the sea serpent "did not appear to avoid anything. He appeared to be amusing himself, though there were several boats not far from him." Ellery was obviously quite taken by the bold stranger who made himself at home in the harbor crowded with Gloucester craft of all sizes.

William H. Foster, a merchant who stood among people seeking a glimpse of the strange creature on August 14, testified to Nash the day after Ellery gave his statement. On August 27 William Foster, the first of the three merchants Nash ultimately deposed, gave his answers about the August 14 sighting. Foster's age is not given but, if he is the William Foster born in Newburyport or the William Foster born in Salisbury, he was in his late thirties. Nash does not clarify what goods Merchant Foster bought and sold. He could have been in the line of middle men who bought fish. They then sold fish in a barrel to a growing country, with some growing rich. Or Foster could have been a ships' chandler, stocking a sea-going vessel with a line of goods such as compasses, sextants, maps, hammocks, hooks, marine chronometers, buckets, scrub brushes, waterproofing grease and tobacco. Perhaps he handled weapons like guns, knives, lead, casting molds, pellets and powder; patent medicines, lineaments and creams; or even hardware like razors, strops, hammers, nails and carpenter's chalk. Haberdashers enjoyed a brisk trade where head protection from wind and sun combined with hat fashions to keep the merchandise moving. As a sideline item in a larger store including stationery and legal forms, ledger books and journals, Foster might have even sold Bibles, Salem mathematician Nathaniel Bowditch's book on navigation, Bigelow's catalogue of Boston flowers, Dr. Rush's treatise on mental illness and British or French novels.

In any case, at some point between sales or at the end of a long day, Foster paused for the sea serpent—or the sea serpent paused for Foster.

"When I discovered him," he told Nash, referring to the sea serpent as everyone did with a masculine pronoun, "his head was above the surface of the water, perhaps ten inches, and he made but little progress through the water."

Foster's limpid sea serpent contrasted against the vigorous one Ellery saw just after sunset, but Nash did not ask Foster the time of his observation.

When the sea serpent did move, however, he exposed to onlookers not only his flexibility but also his gigantic size. Foster detected no pattern. Foster said:

> He afterwards went in different directions, leaving on the surface of the water, marks like those made by skaters on the ice. Then he would move in a straight line west, and would almost in an instant, change his course to east, bringing his head, as near as I could judge, to where his tail was; or in fact, to the extreme hinder part visible, raising himself as he turned, six or eight inches out of the water, and shewing a body at least forty feet in length.

Before more C.L. Sargent witnesses, the reader is asked to stop and recognize one familiar face in the crowd of August 14—the face of Lonson Nash. Nash does not say whether he escorted Nabby to view the remarkable sight. He may not have wanted to frighten her or the children.

In any case, Nash, alone or with his family, brought a spyglass with him on August 14. Nash alluded in his cover letter with his depositions with teasing brevity that he, too, had seen the creature but only after Judge Davis solicited the details.

Many people stood on the rocks or beach around Half Moon Beach, anticipating that the sea serpent would come into or go out of the harbor here, past them. Justice Nash stood among talkative "mariners" in this area, with his spyglass in hand. *Courtesy of Roseanne Cody.*

In his most polite manner, as one gentleman to another, Judge Davis wrote Nash, "It appears by your letter that you had sight of the animal. A letter from you giving a detailed account of your observations would be particularly acceptable."

Nash wrote promptly in reply that, although he and the sea serpent were never closer than a cautious 250 yards of one another, he had his telescope ("glass") and a good view from a hill on shore about 30 feet above the harbor on a day that "the sea was smooth." Standing near Nash was what he termed "seafaring men" who told him that they could distinctly see a head that Nash could not make out. Nash modestly concluded that "they spoke the truth; but not having been much accustomed to look through a glass, I was not so fortunate."

Nash instead described an ocean anaconda.

"I judged him (in the largest part) about the size of a half barrel, gradually tapering towards the two extremes," Nash wrote Judge Davis and the committee. "His colour appeared nearly black—his motion was vertical. When he moved on the surface of the water, the track in his rear was visible for at least half a mile."

The long track followed from his high speed.

"His velocity, when moving on the surface of the water, I judged was at the rate of a mile in about four minutes," Nash estimated. Nash said that he

Stage Fort Park continues to attract both tourists and locals in part because, from rocks and highlands above Half Moon Beach, the view of Gloucester harbor is panoramic. *Courtesy of Manuel Simoes.*

could often trace the sea serpent by disturbance of the surface water when he went under and concluded that he swam "as straight as you could draw a line" even faster and did not swim very deep. "When immersed in the water, his speed was greater, moving, I should say, at the rate of a mile in two or at most three minutes."

As to the serpent's movements in the harbor, Nash described that whenever he changed course his velocity diminished "but little—the two extremes that were visible appeared rapidly moving in opposite directions, and when they came parallel, they appeared not more than a yard apart."

About the animal's length, Nash estimated that he distinctly saw forty-five feet of the sea serpent.

"If he should be taken, I have no doubt that his length will be found seventy feet at least," Nash predicted. "I should not be surprised, if he should be found one hundred feet long."

These were the committee's witnesses. Besides Mrs. Moore, C.L. Sargent's witnesses of August 14 included one standing near Mrs. Moore at Piper's Rocks, four at or near the windmills, two near the Cut at Somes's ropewalk and others near Stage Head, Rocky Neck or Norman's Woe. Sargent's witnesses covered the waterfront.

Jonathan Brown, the one near Mrs. Moore at Piper's Rocks, said succinctly that he saw "60 or 80 of black substance [*sic*] on the water between the beach and Stage Point, many people with glasses all around the shore looking at him, saw him move in a semi-circular form, repeatedly."

Gloucester's Old Fort at Stage Fort Park—usually unoccupied but intermittently manned during the American Revolution, War of 1812 and Civil War—overlooked all of Gloucester harbor. Piper's Rocks are in the harbor just below the fort. As one Mrs. Moore crossed the Cut on August 14, 1817, she saw the sea serpent near Piper's Rocks and was "so alarmed that she trembled like a leaf." *Courtesy of Roseanne Cody.*

Today's Stacy Boulevard was, throughout August 1817, a busy and crowded place through which one would have had to elbow one's way patiently and cautiously to the front in order to get a good view. *Courtesy of Manuel Simoes.*

76

The Tavern Restaurant was built at the end of today's Stacy Boulevard, roughly where two windmills stood in 1817. Sighting the sea serpent from on or near the windmills on August 14, 1817, were C.L. Sargent's informants Captain Davidson, Z. Stevens, William Row and the "Wife of Trask." *Courtesy of Roseanne Cody.*

Almost unnamed among the windmill witnesses, the "Wife of Trask [*sic*]" said with equal brevity that she was at the windmills "with a good glass" and that what she saw "seemed like gallon kegs tied together, saw him suddenly disappear and came up again at a great distance."

Reporting to Sargent in the same concise way, Z. Stevens "from the windmill between the beach and Stage Point" saw the sea serpent "lying on the surface of the water perfectly still, the humps plainly to be seen extending about 50 feet; his head and tail was not visible" although Stevens "had a good glass." Stevens told Sargent that he was confident that "what he saw [was] of the serpent kind: has heard of the horse mackerel, but is confident he could not mistake a fish of that kind for what he saw."

Captain Davidson "near the windmills" with his "good glass" on August 14 said that he saw the creature "60 or 90 feet plain out of water, is certain what he saw was a live substance on the surface and not wake of any fish."

The fourth witness "standing on the windmill point" also with a "good glass," John Lowe—possibly Nash's brother-in-law, Jonathan Lowe's son— told Sargent that he saw the sea serpent "between the beach and Stage Point about two-thirds the way over" and "could plainly distinguish his humps as before described, that he lay perfectly still in the water for some time and,

These wind-borne gulls beside the Tavern Restaurant demonstrate the advantages in this part of the harbor for windmills. *Courtesy of Manuel Simoes.*

On the right side of the Cut Bridge (today the Blynman Bridge), John Somes operated a ropewalk. Somes and Joseph Moores saw the sea serpent from Somes's ropewalk area. *Courtesy of Roseanne Cody.*

as he rose and lowered in the water, he was more distinctly seen at some times than others." Low said emphatically that he was accustomed to seeing objects in the water and "could not mistake it for other than a fish of the serpent kind from 80 to 100 feet."

Standing with others at Stage Head, on the other side of the harbor from these witnesses (today's Stage Fort Park area), Joseph Proctor "saw the serpent from 60 to 80 feet as plain out of water as a rock, saw him still and in motion, saw him repeatedly at different times with the same appearance of humps and at times rapidly in motion."

John Somes, the owner of a ropewalk on the beach at the Cut, standing "just at high water mark" midway between the windmill group and Proctor on Stage Head, saw the sea serpent "pass repeatedly across the harbor and at times he was perfectly still on the water, saw his humps plain but did not count them, saw from 60 to 70 feet of him on the surface of the water; saw his head and neck very plain out of water, and they had every appearance of a Serpent." Somes said that he "could not mistake in describing what he saw" and that he saw him a number of times but "not so plain as on the 14th."

Joseph Moores, an articulate man "standing by Mr. Somes' ropewalk near the beach" (today's Stacy Boulevard) spoke with C.L. Sargent about "a black

As reported by C.L. Sargent, children of Samuel Wonson were so scared that they ran into the house upon seeing the sea serpent "brot up" short just off Norman's Woe on August 14, 1817. *Courtesy of Roseanne Cody.*

substance on the surface of the water about 60 feet long between the beach and Stage Point." Halfway over, Moores said he saw him "put his head near his tail and could plainly see one part of him move one way and the other part in a contrary direction and a continuity of the parts from one end to the other." Exceptional among the watchers, Moores viewed the sea serpent only with his naked eye.

Recounting the most emotional encounter of the day, Samuel Wonson told Sargent that he "saw the serpent between the house and Ten Pound Island, came with great rapidity from Norman's Woe and 'brot to' abreast of me perfectly still at about 100 fathoms distance," which was "so near his children were alarmed and ran into the house."

None of the witnesses directly addressed their motives in being present and watching the sea serpent in large groups for so many hours on August 14. If they had been asked, "Were you waiting and watching for anybody to do anything in particular?" the best-informed among them would likely have answered, "Yes, to see Matthew Gaffney take his best shot." Although that question was not on the committee's list of questions, Matthew Gaffney was on Nash's list of witnesses.

Chapter 10

ONE SHOT

D ocuments from 1817 reflect that August 14 was a special day. The *Boston Patriot* on October 11, 1817, reviewed a panoramic painting of "the TOWN and OUTER HARBOR of GLOUCESTER with the surrounding scenery; the different BOATS, in the position in which they were actually seen on the 14th August, in pursuit of the Monster" amid other ships in the harbor. The review connotes an underlying event, a "pursuit" by specific boats in a scene that was captured by an artist implicitly on site himself, drawn there to draw the kill. When the sea serpent was not killed, the ultimate painting was still produced and put on display as a "pursuit" picture. More distant evidence of minds moving in the same sanguine direction appeared in the *New York Gazette* on August 28, 1817. Unaware of Gaffney's shot, a reporter offered "an expert and accurate rifleman's" advice to "our eastern brethren" on how to deal with the sea serpent: "clap a rifle ball in his eye."

Word around town like that likely gave August 14 a festive holiday atmosphere; Gloucester's several churches may have pealed their bells. Mrs. Moore may have wondered what was going on and decided to cross the Cut bridge. Church bells were the common clock, the fire signal system and the local alarm in New England towns. During the War of 1812, a British frigate fired at steeples not from impiety but in order to disable communication. The cannonball that hit home in the First Parish (Congregational) was hung suspended thereafter from a chain as a war memorial.

Anybody who came to Gloucester to see a sea serpent drama unfold on August 14 was not disappointed. Matthew Gaffney, the observed of observers, surely never had more witnesses watching him hunt any other game. Gaffney's story was worth any number of other stories gathered by Nash. The *Boston Patriot* had it right. Its readers wanted to know about August 14. So would Judge Davis and his committee.

Matthew Gaffney, a skilled laborer, called a ship's carpenter by Nash, was a comparatively young man. Gaffney's garb is not described, no more than that of any other witness; no portrait survives. But he would have been differently dressed than most who saw the sea serpent. He carried a gun and that meant that he had to have an ammunition pouch, probably a hunter's vest of some type and a powder horn or flask. It was a time of black powder and muskets and not cartridges or light-weight arms. Apart from his gear, we can imagine that he wore a hat with a broad brim to cut glare. In a usual workman's all-season wool jersey and baggy pants or even bell-bottom trousers over leather boots greased to be waterproof and probably hobnailed for better footing, Gaffney would have been the Gloucester equivalent of Daniel Boone. Two weeks after August 14, on August 28, Matthew Gaffney gave his statement to Justice Nash. A bachelor who would not marry for another four years, he seems to have been in his early twenties in 1817 and somewhat daring in deed but more conservative in speaking with Justice of the Peace Nash. Unlike witnesses who spoke about a creature whom they *believed* to be a sea serpent, Gaffney gave bolder testimony, referring to what he saw as a "strange marine animal, resembling a serpent."

It was a careful beginning to a story that balanced a tightrope between cosmic stakes behind a strange visitor that might be an instrument of the Lord and the country's glory as Americans seized the moment to advance science. Although Gaffney had seen the creature close up, Nash may have worried that he would be a tight-lipped witness whom he would regret having interviewed. To his relief, Nash found Gaffney's recollections to be vivid. Gaffney was a very good witness who articulated facts well and always refused to speculate about anything that he did not personally see. If he was uncertain about anything, he said so.

Since Gloucester with a sea serpent in its working harbor was Gloucester in a crisis—a crisis resolved only when the sea serpent left—was Matthew Gaffney the one anointed by Gloucester to dispatch the "strange marine animal, resembling a serpent"? Was he expected to take out the sea serpent on August 14? And when he failed, was it to dismay and disappointment? Or was the general reaction "I told you so," among a majority that thought the sea serpent to be indestructible?

Much as a replay of John Josselyn's antique anecdote, Gaffney on August 14 was "in a boat, and was within thirty feet of him." Had it been his own boat, the pronoun "my boat" would surely have been Gaffney's pronoun of choice. In the boat with him were Gaffney's brother, Daniel, and Augustin M. Webber, possibly working sails but more likely—on a day elsewhere reported as calm—rowing.

Even so, if any witness was likely ever to have been hunted down by Nash, it was the hunter of the sea serpent, Matthew Gaffney. Gaffney, of all of the witnesses of all the days, had aimed his weapon at the sea serpent. He spoke on the record to Nash of external events and facts. About any internal drama, the drama of greatest interest to us, Gaffney was mum. The only witness to all of that drama, Gaffney, died without talking.

Nash interviewed both brothers. From Matthew, he got a signed deposition. But he reported to the committee, uniquely, having asked Daniel Gaffney questions off the record. Nash only summarized Daniel's answers in a line. This deviation from protocol was extraordinary. Nash was an experienced member of the bar who well knew that a deposition and a corroborating deposition were much more valuable to the committee than a deposition standing alone or with an off-the-record summary. There may be a reason that Nash did the latter. A demonstrably industrious man interested enough in the sea serpent to be harbor side on August 14, Nash was not lazy or indifferent. A deal may have been struck with the hero of August 14. If Gaffney had been inclined to stay off the record, Nash may have secured his prize witness by agreeing that brother Daniel would only have to answer a few questions and would not be hounded to give or sign a formal statement like Matthew.

Overall, Nash never described any part of the process of witness selection or witness protection. He may have chased some witnesses and begged them to take part. On the other hand, it was the biggest event in Gloucester's history in a long time. Maybe all of Nash's witnesses were unsolicited volunteers or the cream of a bumper crop of witnesses, only the ones who survived the cut.

The plausibility that more people begged Nash to hear their stories than he took the time to hear and write up carefully in sworn depositions arises naturally from C.L. Sargent's abundant collection of statements. Sargent's group may have been Nash's gleanings—stones that Nash had rejected. But Matthew Gaffney was on Nash's list. By whatever means and whatever pressures, Matthew found himself in the company of the town's elite. He joined the small group of merchants, shipowners and sea captains who each, in his turn, sat across the table from Nash.

The justice of the peace asked questions and took down Gaffney's words before he had him swear to and sign to the truth of his statements. It was a remarkable interview on both sides. Nash was stimulated to deviate from the committee's list of questions. No protocol threw Gaffney off. Not nervous but rather in his own element, the savvy hunter told his story concisely and from his angle, neither more nor less.

"His head appeared full as large as a four-gallon keg," Gaffney told Nash, "his body as large as a barrel, and his length that I saw, I should judge forty feet, at the least."

Coming from a ship's carpenter who was used to making measurements, Gaffney's estimates carry special impact.

His brother and Webber seem to have manned the boat in a crowded harbor in support of Gaffney's opportunity for a clear shot. Their attention would have been divided. Daniel and Webber would have had their hands full on August 14. It was not "clear sailing." Instead, navigating the harbor and maneuvering the boat in and around the very center of attraction—the sea serpent—Daniel and Webber kept an active eye on other boats as well as the bulky and balky creature whom sailors feared might capsize their boats and who might be dangerous as a shark or a whale's tail to anybody flailing in the water.

What was the nature of the drama that unfolded when Matthew Gaffney took one shot and missed?

Some facts are clear, facts that Gaffney readily shared with Nash and signed off on for the record. One problem was that the instructions of the committee, the list of questions it gave Nash, were never calculated to ascertain the motivation of a person who took a shot at the animal or who missed. No doubt Nash had questions beyond the committee's short list. It was possible, even likely, that Nash took advantage of his one-on-one to put the additional questions to Gaffney off the record. However, no trace of Gaffney's state of mind survived beyond the rigid deposition and what one can read or sense between the lines of the prime actor's narrative.

Gaffney's deposition was a hunter's narrative of a hunt, at least on its face.

Watching the sea serpent spiral around in some sort of display during which Gaffney discerned that the "top part of his head was of a dark colour, and the under part of his head appeared nearly white, as did also several feet of his belly," Gaffney waited for his chance to kill or disable the beast unknown to science, otherwise known as dinner. Unlike the other deponents, Gaffney wanted the creature at its closest. Probably cradling his weapon in his hands, relaying orders to his brother and to Webber on the course of the boat, rowboat or sailboat, in order to close up any gap between him and his target, self-disciplined Gaffney bided his time to the last second.

"I fired at him, when he was nearest to me," Gaffney said.

He missed.

Or did he?

He said that he was mystified.

He lamented to Nash, "I had a good gun, and took good aim. I aimed at his head, and think I must have hit him."

But, inexplicably, the creature survived.

"He turned toward us immediately after I had fired, and I thought he was coming at us," Gaffney reported, his knuckles possibly white around his gun at the time, "but he sunk down and went directly under our boat, and made his appearance at about one hundred yards from where he sunk."

Gaffney dwelt on that moment.

"He did not turn down like a fish, but appeared to settle directly down, like a rock."

After all, Gaffney, heart in his throat, probably a veteran deer slayer, was watching to see whether his big prey would stumble and fall, if he had brought down the mighty sea serpent with a single, well-aimed, direct shot.

Many witnesses are nondescript. But Gaffney revealed to Nash a marksman's world. The ship's carpenter had weighed out his shot many times before August 14. Today, he would have frequented gun shows and tried out different types of weapons and ammunition.

"My gun carries a ball of eighteen to the pound; and I suppose there is no person in town, more accustomed to shooting, than I am," he told Nash. It was a modest boast coming from one who at that time held the world title of "The Man Most Accustomed to Shooting Sea Serpents."

As a vignette on daily life in 1817, Matthew Gaffney illustrated how any unlicensed, carefree spirit could buy or borrow and carry a gun to sea, to work or to hunt in Dogtown. Whether Gaffney always carried his gun is not clear. He may have always hoped to drop a duck or a goose flying overhead as he went his rounds. In any case, the ship's carpenter on somebody else's boat broke no rules. Regardless of whether he was expected to be the hero of the day, he was in no danger in any case of being stopped from bringing his "good gun" aboard any of Gloucester's vessels. Whatever boat Gaffney rode, his weapon raised no red flags— especially during sea serpent hunting season.

Gaffney's "good gun" exemplifies another thing about 1817 and the early days of manufacturing. Mass production did not result in uniformly good products. Gaffney called the product that he had tested and found it to be "good." He vouched for his weapon personally. Although there were gunsmiths, Gloucester was not overall a hunting community likely to support one. Gaffney, a retailer or person before him, probably purchased this "good gun" directly or indirectly from a factory along the Connecticut River, in Springfield, Massachusetts, or Hartford, Connecticut. In short, when he spoke of possessing a "good gun" presumably made in America and presumably fairly new, Matthew Gaffney of Gloucester was casually and incidentally expressing national pride.

Although Gaffney's statements about the sea serpent depict him as both playful and brave, the hunter nonetheless plainly regretted having missed making a fatal mark on him at close range. He told Nash, "I have seen the same animal at several other times, but never had so good a view of him, as on this day."

Gaffney's short remark intensifies the possibility—let's adopt Gaffney's favorite adjective and make it a "good" possibility—that boats converged in force around the "monster" with a plan formed before the pursuers set out. It appears that it was no accident or bit of good luck that Gaffney had the best view of all attending, his own best view ever, in order that he might take his best shot. Context is useful to understand this probability. Gloucester was a small town of perhaps 1,500 people. Gaffney's superior skill as a marksman would have been known. Others, even any who carried weapons, deferred to the expert as the designated hit man.

Gaffney probably shouted on the scene to others that he had hit him.

Accordingly, when the creature rose back up from his instantaneous dive, he probably resurfaced to a suddenly empty harbor.

By implication of his own statement that the sea serpent surfaced a hundred yards from where he dove, Gaffney's boat was no longer near. The entire fleet of boats likely scattered in an immediate and intentional maneuver not to be anywhere near a wounded, large and fast sea serpent. It was déjà vu of Josselyn's anecdotal snake all over again; "if he were not kill'd outright, they would be all in danger of their lives." As soon as he shot and the smoke cleared, Gaffney likely took fright himself. As he told Nash the story, he thought that the sea serpent was coming at him before it unexpectedly dove. Coming at him?! Gaffney rested quite satisfied after one unsuccessful shot.

Nash avoided this sensitive point. Rather than reflect anything adverse or humiliating about the pursuers in a panic caught up in a rush away from the sea serpent that they had been pursuing, Nash asked nothing about the pursuers pursued. It was easy, given Nash's short list of questions, presumably on the table before him or in his hands to be read aloud, question by question. Nash talked with Gaffney about August 14 with extreme caution. His focus was on the sea serpent. But, near the end of their interview, Nash asked Gaffney, "Did he appear more shy, after you had fired at him?"

The question was perhaps tongue-in-cheek. After all, Nash had been in "the front row" ashore with his telescope and, even if his view had been temporarily obscured by sails or he had been caught up by a sudden crowd surge, Nash would have heard all about the retreat. Nash would have known whether the sea serpent got shy—or his pursuers did.

Gaffney may have smiled at Nash when he answered in eight words, "He did not; but continued playing as before."

Gaffney said nothing about trying another shot or about the other boats for the obvious reason that the pursuers left the prey to play. Nash was happy with the one question. Gaffney, for his part, exhibited an ungrudging respect for the creature who, shot at by him at close range and surely hit, only "continued playing as before."

For Judge Davis's purposes, Gaffney did more than narrate his single shot. Like Foster, helpfully for the judge's committee, Gaffney confirmed that the sea serpent's motion "was vertical, like the caterpillar." Given his view within thirty feet and a hunter's close attention to the motions of the animal in his sights, Gaffney's confirming words are important.

In terms of speed, Gaffney felt that the sea serpent could move at "the rate of a mile in two, or at most, three minutes."

About what was for him a target, Gaffney was solicited to answer the committee's texture question: smooth or rough? The hunter, extremely concerned with the movement of his prey, had no professional reason to consider texture.

"I thought it smooth," he answered, "though I was endeavoring to take aim at him, and will not say positively that he was smooth, though that is still my belief."

Again on locomotion and again corroborating Foster, Gaffney spoke of the sea serpent making his turns "quick and short, and the first part of the curve that he makes in turning, is in the form of the staple; but his head seems to approach rapidly towards his body, his head and tail moving in opposite directions, and when his head and tail come parallel, they appear almost to touch each other."

Neither Daniel Gaffney nor Augustin M. Webber testified. Nash gives no reason for their omission from his list of witnesses. Obviously, these men had likewise seen the sea serpent within thirty feet. Nash spoke with Daniel, apparently after he had interviewed Matthew and apparently off the record.

"I have questioned Daniel Gaffney," Nash told the committee in his cover letter ("Gaffney" was misprinted as "Goffney" in the book later). Nash verified that Daniel "was in the boat with his brother Matthew, when he fired at the animal, and Daniel's answers corroborate Matthew's testimony."

It is strange.

There may have been an informal election.

Perhaps Daniel Gaffney and Augustin M. Webber elected Matthew as the boat's spokesman because he had the best and longest view of the sea serpent or because he was the best speaker and would make the best witness. Perhaps Daniel was the younger brother. A slight clue indicates Augustin M. Webber's possible relationship with the Gaffneys. Matthew Gaffney married Henrietta Webber on November 15, 1822. They had ten children who survived, about one every two years. Matthew's brother and Augustin, his future father-in-law or brother-in-law, may have had personal reasons to defer to Matthew and not to testify.

Although many important questions remained unanswered and neither of his sidekicks spoke on the record, Gaffney's interview was Nash's best. Nash extracted from him information of more use to the committee than from any other witness while, at the same time, he negotiated around the rock of embarrassment latent in the turn of events and turn of the boats of August 14. Gloucester could breathe a collective sigh of relief. Gaffney's verbal snapshots reflect August 14 in a craftily edited way. Meaty with quite specific and plainly spoken facts, the Matthew Gaffney deposition did Gloucester history good. Gaffney hit the high points of August 14 and missed any low point. Gaffney was allowed or led to celebrate the worthy creature that the town's heroic and intrepid best marksman could not bring down with a clear shot fired by a good gun at close range. Any panic among the pursuers remained between the lines, hidden, unstated and obscure, behind the figure of the doughty sea serpent that "played" in Gloucester harbor *after* just as he did *before* Gaffney's one shot.

Chapter 11

MANSFIELD'S SIGHTING

August 15

James Mansfield, merchant, testified concisely. What he bought and sold as a merchant does not appear in the record. Was Mansfield a small-time storekeeper? Did pepper, salt, sugar and spices make up a good part of his inventory? Or did Mansfield stand in the center of a global commercial network of codfish, slaves, rum, molasses, ships and real estate? There is no telling today. James Mansfield stood somewhere in the spectrum of merchants between the largest and smallest and richest and poorest. He may have been a porcupine type who knew one thing and did it well, or a fox with his fingers in many pies. But if his word count reflects his way of life, Mansfield was frugal. He spared few words. Mansfield had few details to offer, none of them new; although one of those who had seen the sea serpent multiple times, weirdly, he seemed to have never had a good view.

He spoke of August 15 as his best sighting ever. It took place as shadows lengthened over the harbor, "a little before six o'clock P.M." Not at noon on a bright day but a couple of hours before the sun goes down over Gloucester in mid-August, Mansfield saw the sea serpent. He was swimming an estimated 180 yards from where Mansfield stood on shore. With Nash, Mansfield attempted to estimate the creature's size and give other general details within his limits.

Immediately referring to the size of the creature, Mansfield told Nash, "I should say he was from forty to sixty feet in length, extended on the surface of the water, with his head above the water about a foot. He remained in this position but a short time, and then started off very quick, with much greater velocity than I have seen him move at any other time."

Words, of course, are where experiences go to die. The transcribed event is but the dried, scummy residue of the once-real and three-dimensional. Much of the sea serpent's life had been sucked out of it before Mansfield, judging from his wording as reported by Nash, likely spoke in crisp diction. No harm, really, but Mansfield transcribed comes across like a gentleman who would pronounce his consonants carefully and who would doubtless look you straight in the eye as he spoke, to ascertain your understanding of what he was communicating. Hopefully, he made a better businessman than he made a sea serpent witness.

"I saw bunches on his back about a foot in height, when he lay extended on the water," Mansfield said. He offered nothing more about those "bunches." Despite the committee's routine question of how many distinct portions were out of the water at one time, Nash recorded no such thing. He seems not to have asked that question. Perhaps the answer lies in Nash's cover letter. He assured the committee that its questions "were all put to the witnesses; but generally, I have omitted inserting them in the deposition, when the witnesses declared their inability to answer them." If asked, then Mansfield answered that he did not know how many bunches he saw.

Mansfield was vague also about the sea serpent's color, which he described as "black, or very dark."

In reply to Nash's question, "Were its sinuosities vertical, or horizontal?" and in common with almost all witnesses, Mansfield said one word: "Vertical."

Only when Mansfield wrestled to describe the head of the sea serpent did he finally speak at any length. Even then, Mansfield had a very poor idea of what that head looked like. He felt that he had to say what he had not seen, and why.

"His head appeared to be about the size of the crown of a hat, at the distance from whence I saw him," Mansfield recalled. Straining through false starts, he told Nash, "The shape of his head I cannot describe; and I saw no ears, horns, or other appendages. I had no spy-glass, and cannot describe him so minutely as I otherwise could."

Mansfield seemed fairly to writhe. He basically excused himself for being a flat failure as a sea serpent witness. With his parting sentence, he invoked how any observer's perceptive possibilities varied. Some saw more of the sea serpent, others less, at greater distances, without a glass. He had tried. Of the fifteenth, he said, probably with a shrug of his shoulders, palms extended, "I have seen him at other times, but my view of him was not so good, as on this day."

Chapter 12

FOSTER'S AND JOHNSTON'S SIGHTINGS

August 17

On August 17, when Mansfield's fellow Gloucester merchant William H. Foster got luckier than Mansfield, at least in the field of sea serpentology, Nash gratefully deposed Foster on his second sighting of the sea serpent, which was a lulu.

Foster said:

> *On the seventeenth of August instant, I again saw him. He came into the harbor, occasionally exhibiting parts of his body, which appeared like rings or bunches. As he drew near, and when opposite to me, there rose from his head or the most forward part of him, a prong or spear about twelve inches in height, and six inches in circumference at the bottom, and running to a small point.*

Nash could not resist. He deviated from the committee's script. Putting aside the questions he had from Boston, Nash simply had to inquire closely about the unicorn-of-the-sea that Foster claimed to have seen. Nash cross examined.

"Might not the prong or spear that you saw, have been the tongue of the serpent?" the justice asked Foster. Pointedly, Nash was not inclined to buy the merchant's story.

Sticking to his story at first, Foster said, "I thought not; as I saw the prong before I saw the head." Perhaps after a pause, in any case next, he added, presumably nervously and possibly thinking about the oath he would swear to before signing his statement, "but it might have been."

Nash, successful with his first foray into a conditional admission, tried one more lob. He asked Foster in old lawyer-grammar, "At what distance was you, when you saw the spear of the serpent."

Foster distanced himself.

"I should judge forty rods; I had a spy-glass when I saw the prong or spear."

The spear or prong, of course, may have been tossed harpoonlike into the animal's head on or after August 14. It may not have been noticed by others before Mansfield and it may have fallen off shortly afterward. Note that Foster himself called it a "prong or spear." Old whales have been found with harpoons in their sides from attacks made on them decades earlier. But Nash had had enough of that part of Foster's story and resumed the committee's questions. Foster ended up almost monosyllabically racing through his answers: yes, the sea serpent did appear round; yes, it did appear jointed; its sinuosities were vertical; it appeared to be brown; and it appeared to be smooth.

As was the case for Mansfield, Foster had some detail trouble with the head. Despite having seen the prong or spear through his spyglass, the head "appeared as large as a man's head, but I cannot describe its shape."

Foster said that the sea serpent "appeared to notice objects," which was a skill he could only be said to reach himself in occasional gusts of lucidity.

As to speed, "a mile a minute" was Foster's estimate, a calculation of which he somehow had "no doubt."

Although Nash vouched to the committee that all of the persons deposed before him were "men of fair and unblemished character," Foster was not one of the two prize witnesses—Gaffney and Pearson—whose names Nash especially denominated for the committee's attention. Nor did Nash name for the committee's close scrutiny the account of John Johnston Jr., all of seventeen years old, the only minor who testified.

When Nash spoke with Johnston, he engaged for the first time with fear. His earlier sturdy, stalwart deponents had inspired Nash's best Jack Webb style, just the facts—objective, sterile, scientific. But, as he spoke with Johnston, the father in Nash came out, as he dealt with an emotion that was only latent in other observers but rose clearly to the surface when Johnston spoke and looked at Nash. Whether it was Johnston's youth or Nash's paternal skill that led Johnston to speak freely, Nash deviated from his practice of questions and answers in favor of a summary. The summary format itself hints at how difficult, how rambling and how piecemeal the restless boy's account of a traumatic experience was. No reader today can avoid an impression of a young man speaking about an event that still affected him. It seems, in a word, that Johnston thought that he had narrowly evaded death.

Johnston, perhaps stammering, certainly nervous and his evening observation doubtless obscured by darkness, probably could not have answered most of the committee's questions. Nash, using his own vocabulary and formal grammar, summarized Johnston's experience. As drafted by Nash and published in seventeen lines, Johnston's brief encounter ran as follows:

> *On the evening of the seventeenth day of August, A.D. 1817, between the hours of eight and nine o'clock, while passing from the shore in a boat, to a vessel lying in the harbour in said Gloucester, I saw a strange marine animal, that I believe to be a serpent, lying extended on the surface of the water. His length appeared to be fifty feet at least, and he appeared straight, exhibiting no protuberances.* [One must acknowledge that this term was more likely Nash's rather than the lad's!] *Capt. John Corliss and George Marble were in the boat with me. We were within two oars length of him, when we discovered him, and were rowing directly for him. We immediately rowed from him, and at first concluded to pass by his tail; but fearing we might strike it with the boat, concluded to pass around his head, which we did, by altering our course. We approached so near to him that I believe I could have reached him with my oar. There was not sufficient light to enable me to describe the animal.*

The long, straight and motionless item floating in the harbor without "protuberances" was scary, indeed. But was it a sea serpent or a log? Did Captains Corliss and Marble have some fun in considering whether to go around the "tail" or the "head" of a shape that they may have well understood to be nothing more than wood? In any case, neither Corliss nor Marble testified. Nor did Nash appear to consult with either one. The lad's statement, while on its face the closest encounter possible, an oar's length from the rower, while of no value whatever to the Davis committee, nonetheless today allows the reader to discern between the lines that, in Gloucester, after Gaffney's shot, at least at night, at least among young men or boys of the waterfront, the reaction to the sea serpent—even the sea serpent at rest or dead—was one of fear.

Captain Corliss, reached later by C.L. Sargent, made a statement that corroborated Johnston. Captain Corliss told Sargent (who spelled his name "Corlis" but this was just careless) that he was that day "in a boat between the fort [today, above Half Moon Beach] and Ten Pound Island" when he "plainly saw the serpent lying still on the surface at the distance of about 30 feet." "Apprehensive of being too near him," Captain Corliss "immediately rowed from him, [but] his noise alarmed the serpent and he made off with great speed." Captain Corliss was certain that he saw "40 feet of him out of water or, rather, lying on the surface" and was "certain he could not mistake him for any than a strange fish of the serpent kind."

William Saville told C.L. Sargent that he saw the sea serpent on the afternoon of August 17, while standing near the windmill, when "something appeared above the water from 40 to 50 feet long in distinct bunches but, soon after, being alarmed by the noise on shore, he sunk in the water."

Saville's final, lugubrious words were, "We saw him no more."

Saville only spoke for himself. More sightings in Gloucester were reported.

Chapter 13

PEARSON'S SIGHTING

August 18

"I saw Mr. Gaffney fire at him," William B. Pearson told Nash at his deposition on August 27. He estimated that Gaffney was about thirty yards from the sea serpent.

"I thought he hit him," Pearson said, affirming Gaffney's own opinion. He then deviated from Gaffney in opining that after the shot "he appeared more shy."

In his cover letter Nash invited the committee's attention to two witnesses in particular: to the testimony of Matthew Gaffney, the young ship carpenter, and to the testimony of William B. Pearson, a Gloucester merchant.

Curiously, Pearson's best sighting was not of the shot-then-shy serpent of August 14 (when Nash, too, viewed the creature). Pearson said that he made his best sighting afterward, on August 18. Speaking about August 18 with Nash scarcely a week later, Pearson's fresh account is, on its face, the most valuable of the depositions. Nash rightly invited committee attention to it. Unlike Gaffney, whose observations were made under pressure on an exciting day before crowds, of a creature with which he was engaged in struggle—hunter and hunted, before the tables turned—Pearson made a good sighting under ideal conditions.

Pearson declared modestly of his several sea serpent sightings, "I have had a good view of him, only once, and this was on the 18th of August, A.D. 1817."

Pearson said that he was in a small sailboat with James P. Collins. Nash's summary of occupation, the one word "merchant," could cover a mobile merchant—the merchant typified a century later by Captain Ben Pine, who sailed about the harbor with merchandise and supplies, selling items from boat to boat. Whether he had a store on shore, Pearson was literally a merchant on water at the time of his "good view" on August 18. As the harbor breeze moved their craft along off Webber's Cove, Pearson saw "something coming out of the cove."

"We hove to, not doubting but that it was the same creature that had been seen several times in the harbour," Nash wrote, transcribing what Pearson told him.

As the two men on the sailboat watched, the serpent "passed out under the stern of our boat, towards Ten Pound Island; then he stood in towards us again, and crossed our bow."

Even after being shot or at least shot at, and his brief reputed period of withdrawal or shyness, by August 18 the sea serpent was as curious about the two men in the sailboat as they were about him.

In a reluctant and implicit way, like young Johnston's narrative summary, Pearson's extensive and detailed report is by an observer who was not merely curious and excited but also scared.

"We immediately exclaimed, 'here is the snake!'" Pearson said. "From what I saw of him, I should say that he was nothing short of seventy feet in length. I distinctly saw bunches on his back, and once he raised his head out of water. The top of his head appeared flat, and was raised seven or eight inches above the surface of water."

The men kept a careful eye to see where, exactly, he was going, although Pearson had time enough and presence of mind to make a quick count of the "bunches," which he thought amounted to ten or twelve distinct portions. Pearson then became Gloucester's only "eye" witness. That the sea serpent had eyes, even if only sharp slit-like dark apertures, was apparent but that was still more than any of the Gloucester deponents before Pearson would swear to or sign. Pearson thought that he and the sea serpent made eye contact. It must have been brief, a passing glance. And it must have been unnerving. In the ongoing anxious chaos, when the head came up in view, Pearson said, he "thought and believed" that he "saw his eye at one time, and it was dark and sharp."

Gaffney's shot may have slowed the sea serpent down.

"He passed by the bow of the boat, at about thirty yards distance," Pearson said, "His colour was a dark brown. I saw him at this time about two minutes. His motion was vertical. His velocity at this time was not great; though at times, I have seen him move with great velocity, I should say at the rate of a mile in three minutes, and perhaps faster."

He judged his circumference to be "about the size of a half barrel." As any Gloucester merchant would be familiar with barrels and measuring stock at a distance, Pearson's estimate is highly credible.

One last item from Pearson is slightly uncertain. Although Nash rarely made a narrative difficult to follow, it is confusing whether Pearson was describing the sea serpent on August 14 or on August 18. If the following belongs to Pearson's best sighting, it dated from August 18, between 5 and 6 o'clock in the afternoon:

> *He turned very short, and appeared as limber and active as an eel, when compared to his size. The form of the curve when he turned in the water, resembled a staple; his head seemed to approach towards his body for some feet; then his head and tail appeared moving rapidly, in opposite directions, and when his head and tail were on parallel lines, they appeared not more than two or three yards apart.*

In conclusion, at the tail-end of Pearson's report, he answered Nash's question, "How did its tail terminate?"

Pearson said, "I had not a distinct view of his tail; I saw no bunches towards, what I thought, the end of his tail, and I believe there were none. From where I judged his navel might be to the end of his tail, there were no bunches visible."

Note that Pearson was not saying that he saw the creature's bellybutton. He only spoke about the midpoint of the long creature or where he "judged his navel might be."

Nash was right to invite the committee's attention especially to Pearson's deposition. Pearson's account is the most satisfying in detail although no mere sighting could surpass Gaffney's dramatic account of an encounter.

Chapter 14
STORY'S LAST SIGHTING

August 23

Although Nash sent Judge Davis the Ten Pound Island "log" story of August 22, when Amos Story's wife said that she saw a log, or perhaps the sea serpent motionless, through a glass from home on the edge of the island and, when she looked later, discovered it gone, Nash started with Story and ended with Story, the same old Story, the one who had first seen the sea serpent on Sunday, August 10, who saw it again on the morning he testified to Nash on August 23, and thus became the Gloucester witness last recorded as having seen its sea serpent of 1817.

Full circle, Story told Nash about his sighting from about 7 o'clock that morning. Where, on August 10, Story had marveled at the speed and grace of the sea serpent doing turns in the harbor, on August 23, he saw the sea serpent forty rods away from him and his "good spy-glass," lying "perfectly still, extended on the water," in position for Story to see what he estimated as "fifty feet of him."

"I continued looking at him about half an hour," Story said. His option of watching a sea serpent through his spyglass for a half-hour at about 7 in the morning hammered home the same old point that 1817 was no time-clock world. Saturdays were as much workdays as all the other days of the week. Only the Sabbath, Sunday, was a holiday. Nonetheless, the yoke of any mariner was loosely borne. It was possible for any of the sturdy workmen of the harbor to bid their ostensible boss hold off while he attended to satisfying his curiosity or attended a deposition for science.

What Story studied was an inert body.

"He remained still and in the same position, until I was called away," Story told Nash, perhaps at the end of his workday, possibly by candlelight, certainly before the Sabbath started and depositions would be prohibited by the blue laws. That morning, presumably, Story's boss had been patient only to a certain point with the no-longer-novel business of sea serpent sightings until time and tide would not wait. The hook that the fishing industry had in each of the workmen was pulled taut on Story after his self-declared half-hour of leisure. "Neither his head nor his tail were visible," Story said in conclusion. "His colour appeared to be a dark brown, and when the sun shone upon him, the reflection was very bright. I thought his body was about the size of a man's body."

That last comment by Story was about the only physiologically anthropomorphic aspect that could possibly be said of a serpent-like marine creature over fifty feet long with smooth, shiny skin, whose locomotion was faster than anything that large on or under the sea, a mile in less than three minutes. It was not like a man nor was it very like a whale. It was its own animal, unique and unknown to science.

Lonson Nash probably looked over the several signed depositions with a third eye, imagining them to be treasures read by scientists the world over. None of the manuscripts survived. We do not know anything about the looks of a Nash deposition. We do not know if neat, tiny letters in straight rows with uniform margins characterized Nash's documents. Did Nash have good vision or was he myopic? Did his lettering reflect visual difficulty in large letters of the flourishing "John Hancock" hand of the more flamboyant penman? We cannot determine whether anything was crossed out, blotted, inserted or misread when published. Were the depositions even written on stationery of the same size or an assortment? And did Nash use a red wax seal? Whatever they looked like, these manuscripts were Nash's favorite verbal children. He hoped to win fame with them by proxy. Nash, as a final duty, would have fussed over a plan for their prompt, safe passage to Judge Davis.

Was it relief or *tristesse* that Nash felt as he, Nabby, his most trusted son or daughter or all of them together—like the Waltons—folded, tied, sealed and addressed the package? It was a moment of termination, nearly the end of his connection with the committee, the conclusion of his duties for Judge Davis, a man who had sworn in a vice president of the United States.

Much that is automated or mechanized now was then done by hand. Mail did not mean placing an envelope or package into a mailbox. The post office was for newspapers and a few letters. Things like depositions and little black snakes were carried by hand.

Nash likely personally selected a courier. To ensure speedy, correct delivery, Nash would have tagged someone going to Boston whom he knew and trusted. He would have hand carried his packet to someone's office, the stage depot, a home, stable or another rendezvous point in Gloucester to clinch an agreement about bringing the dozen or twenty folded or rolled-and-ribbon-tied pages to Boston. One readily imagines a compact, folded or sealed packet, possibly bound with string or maybe wrapped in a cloth as a buffer against dust, rain or mud in transit, for the irreplaceable and important documents.

Imagine Judge Davis, off the bench, his black robe on a hanger, seated at his chambers desk in shirtsleeves and the windows open for a little air when his clerk tapped on the doorway to announce that a messenger from Gloucester had arrived with a packet of papers.

"Bring him in, by all means!" or some similar words would have come from Davis. His ambitions to have a bundle of sworn, signed statements imminently to be realized, he would have been confident now of a book and of immediate controversy and lasting fame. Now, New Englanders—New England Federalists at that and Judge Davis most visibly included—would make the mark that would put the United States on the map of scientific progress. How do you like that, Mr. Jefferson?

Chapter 15
THE *Laura* SIGHTINGS

August 28

Unexpectedly, the Davis committee found itself hearing three witnesses in Boston who had sighted the sea serpent on Thursday, August 28, from the schooner *Laura* of Newburyport as it passed Eastern Point, Gloucester, outside the harbor.

Their statements' value was enhanced by two factors. First, their memories were recent. The men spoke to the committee only two or three days after the sightings, on August 30 and September 1. Secondly, these witnesses, unlike the eight who took oath before Lonson Nash, had not intermingled with Gloucester witnesses—not that they did not shout their stories from the rooftops once they got to Boston. Some sort of noise led the committee members to solicit their attendance for depositions.

The committee's depositions were conducted hastily and along different lines than their protocol for Lonson Nash. Among other things, there is no way to tell whether the committee went by or ignored the list of twenty questions it had sent to Nash. Questions and answers of the *Laura* witnesses were not transcribed. The *Laura* depositions were mostly notarized by Justice of the Peace Joseph May, but not all three of them. He apparently had to leave before notarizing the statement of one, Robert Bragg, who signed under the affirmation that he was "willing to make oath" to his account. Accordingly, one or both of the legal members of the committee, Judge Davis or Attorney Gray, rather than Doctor Bigelow, likely prepared the one-page accounts, cogent summaries that were peppered with legalese.

No Gloucester sightings were made after the crew of the *Laura*, sailing past Salt Island off Brace's Cove on Eastern Point, observed the sea serpent heading for deeper waters of the Atlantic on August 28, 1817. *Courtesy of Roseanne Cody.*

Sewall Toppan, master of the *Laura*, was clear about the time and place of the sighting. It occurred "at about 9 o'clock A.M. at about two miles, or two and half miles east of the eastern point of Cape Ann."

The schooner, dependent on the winds, floated becalmed.

"I heard one of my men call to the man at the helm, 'what is this coming towards us?'"

Toppan was busy, if not annoyed.

"Being engaged forward I took no further notice till they called out again—I then got on top of the deck load, at which time I saw a singular kind of animal or fish, which I had never seen before, passing by our quarter, at a distance of about forty feet, standing along shore," he told the committee. If he was standing on top of cargo, boxes or barrels, the schooner was apparently fully loaded for its run to Boston.

Toppan forgot about any other work at this point. He devoted all attention to something utterly new.

"I saw part of the animal or fish ten or fifteen feet from the head downwards, including the head," Toppan said "the head appeared to be the size of ten-gallon keg, and six inches above the surface of the water. It was of a dark colour."

Although he saw no tongue, he heard his two men, Robert Bragg and William Somerby, call out "look at his tongue."

He discounted his own impressions on that score. Toppan noted to the committee of the sea serpent, especially its head, that he "saw him much less time than either of the others, and not in so favourable a position to notice his head." For his own part, he modestly observed only that "the motion of his head was sideways and quite moderate; the motion of his body, up and down." Using the measurements with which he was fluently familiar, Toppan judged the body of the animal was about the size of a half barrel in circumference. The man responsible for the safety of the *Laura* and its small crew was attentive that the odd creature "did not appear to alter his course in consequence of being so near the vessel." He did not speak of the relief he must have felt when he passed by the *Laura* on its way to deep sea.

Finally, one may picture a point at which the captain put both hands flat on the writing table on which one of the committee members was scribbling what he said with ink and quill pen. By some body language, perhaps raising himself back to face them or looking Judge Davis straight in the eye, he emphasized the *bona fides* of what he was telling them.

"I have seen whales very often; his motion was much more rapid than whales, or any other fish I have ever seen; he left a very long wake behind him," Toppan said.

"I have been to sea many years, and never saw any fish that had the least resemblance to this animal."

When Robert Bragg, mariner, testified in his turn, he estimated the time as about 10 o'clock in the morning, when the *Laura*, "bound for Newburyport to Boston," lay becalmed about a mile and a half off the shore of Gloucester's Eastern Point.

"I being on deck," Bragg said, "the vessel being becalmed, looking at the windward, I saw something break the water, and coming very fast towards us."

Although Bragg only said that he "mentioned" it to the man at the helm, William Somerby, he said it with such alarm and loudly enough that Toppan could hear his cry below decks. The large animal was at least heading toward the *Laura*, if it was not on a collision course. Bragg's "mention" belongs more aptly to the vocabulary of witnesses ashore who were idly curious about the animal. Bragg's concern was much more mundane, the safety of the small, becalmed and heavily-laden schooner, more than a mile from shore, in days without radio distress signals.

"The animal came about 28 to 30 feet from us, between the vessel and the shore" Bragg said, probably anxious, if not terrified of the possibilities this presented, but it "passed very swiftly by us; he left a very long wake behind him."

Bragg was in a good position to observe and make note of details as the unusual creature sped by.

About six inches in height of his body and head were out of the water, and as I should judge about 14 or 15 feet in length. He had a head like a serpent, rather larger than his body and rather blunt; did not see his eyes; when astern of the vessel about 30 feet, he threw out his tongue about two feet in length; the end of it appeared to me to resemble a fisherman's harpoon; he raised his tongue several times perpendicularly, or nearly so, and let it fall again. He was in sight about ten minutes.

Probably at the committee's request for an estimate, Bragg told them, "I think he moved at the rate of 12 to 14 miles an hour."

As noted, that was a terrific speed for any animal, and few human beings moved that fast in 1817 unless they were falling off a cliff.

Transparently, the rest of his summarized testimony amounted to a series of his answers to committee questions about the sea serpent's color, shape, any noise it made, its "rough or smooth" texture and any other details Bragg recalled.

"He was of a dark chocolate colour, and from what appeared out of the water, I should suppose he was about two and a half feet in circumference; he made no noise; his back and body appeared smooth; a small bunch on each side of his head, just above his eyes; he did not appear to be at all disturbed by the vessel."

With no seeming hesitation or doubt, the experienced sailor vetted out the sea serpent's course for the committee.

"His course was in the direction for the Salt Islands," he said. "His motion was much swifter than any whale I have ever seen, and I have seen many— did not observe any teeth, his motion being very steady, a little up and down."

William Somerby, the *Laura's* helmsman, had occupational reasons to pay attention to passing sea creatures but no leisure to observe them to the exclusion of his duties as helmsman, which froze him in place at the wheel.

Somerby prosaically described their position at 10 o'clock on the morning of August 28 as "off Brace's Cove, a little eastward of Eastern Point [Cape Ann], about two miles from land, the sea calm."

His wording reflected a person at home in calm or stormy seas, an unflappable type who was good at his job and not inclined to tell tales to federal judges.

He told the Davis committee how Robert Bragg had asked him "if that was not a snake coming, pointing out a break in the water, south of us; a strange animal of the serpent form [that] passed very swiftly by us—the nearest distance I should judge to be between 30 and 40 feet—the upper part of his back and head was above water—the length that appeared was about 12 or 15 feet, his head was like a serpent's, tapering off to a point."

Bragg, too, saw the serpent's "tongue."

"He threw out his tongue a number of times, extended about two feet from his jaws," Somerby said. Like Bragg, he thought its end resembled a harpoon.

"He threw his tongue backwards several times over his head, and let it fall again," Somerby said. Of the eight who testified in Gloucester, only one, Pearson, had claimed to have seen the sea serpent's eyes. Somerby later offered an additional nugget: "the colour of his tongue was a light brown."

But the most startling revelation Somerby had for the committee was his vision of the sea serpent's eye.

"I saw one of his eyes as he passed," Somerby said. The committee must have listened keenly, noting each word carefully as he told them one of the rarest of descriptions. Even people who got good views of the sea serpent typically did not sight any eye. By contrast, Somerby told the committee that the eye "appeared very bright, and about the size of the eye of an ox."

In 1817, oxen were the common beasts of heavy burden, yoked in pairs, and even pairs of pairs, sometimes forming a longer train. The steady but slow strong-limbed horned animals were chiefly used to haul the largest wagons full of hay, granite blocks and uncut timber. Anyone on the streets of Newburyport or other seaports, not excluding Boston, would have been familiar with the eye of an ox at close range.

"The color of all that appeared was very dark, almost black," Somerby said, clearly identifying himself as the person who had taken the best view of the sea serpent's eye.

Like Bragg, and likely in reply to the same questions by the committee's members, Somerby said of the sea serpent that he "did not appear to take any notice of the vessel, and made no noise. There appeared a bunch above the eye—should judge him to be about two and a half feet in circumference."

The committee tried to obtain a comparison with whales.

Somerby said that he had often seen whales at sea.

"The motion of this animal was much swifter than any whale. The motion of the body was rising and falling as he advanced, the head moderately vibrating from side to side," he told the committee, as if ticking off in seconds several distinctions between what he saw, the most wonderful of strange animals, and any whale anywhere. The world was full of such a number of things, and Somerby implied that he had now seen them all, including a sea serpent, just off Eastern Point, outside Gloucester harbor.

Chapter 16

THE COMMITTEE TIES UP
THE THREADS

Judge Davis's committee seemed to be leading a charmed life. During the two weeks following its formation on August 18, the committee itself unexpectedly heard witnesses on August 30 and September 1 and statements from the crew of the *Laura* were prepared and signed just as Nash's August 28 letter, wrapping up his Gloucester depositions, was on its way. On September 1, Judge Davis took pleasure in writing his brother, Samuel Davis, of these developments.

"The committee have procured evidence from Gloucester," the judge crowed to Samuel with obvious satisfaction, "which they are prepared to report to the Society, and this evidence is of such a character, that they have thought it expedient to extend their inquiry to other reported appearances of a similar nature on our coasts."

As evidenced by judicial notebooks at the National Archives in Waltham, Judge Davis's handwriting was a tiny, neat, legible script. The judge consistently and economically fitted his content margin to margin with little space between the lines. Decipherment of the judge's request presented no difficulty. Brother Samuel gathered instantly, and correctly, that the judge was interested in the Finney sighting of two or three years earlier.

Apologizing for delay, Samuel replied on October 2 and sent the judge that requested prize, a "deposition duly authenticated of Captain Elkanah Finney of this town, descriptive of an unusual animal." Captain Finney, whom Samuel vouched for as not having read "whatever he may have heard" of descriptions of the Gloucester sea serpent, a seafarer all of his life who had "frequently seen whales, and almost every species of fish" during foreign voyages, had seen the sea serpent without leaving the front yard of his house "situated near the sea shore in Plymouth, at a place called Warren's Cove."

Before inviting Judge Davis's attention to Captain Finney's deposition, Samuel mentioned having talked to carpenters at work on a house near Finney's own who had seen the sea serpent and, he found, "these persons dwell with emphasis on the long and distinct wake made in the water by the passage of the fish."

Captain Finney provided a much longer account than anyone had either from Gloucester or the *Laura*.

"My son, a boy," the captain said, "came from the shore and informed me of an unusual appearance on the surface of the sea in the cove. I paid little attention to his story at first; but as he persisted in saying that he had seen something very remarkable, I looked towards the cove."

What appeared to be drift sea weed about a quarter-mile from shore to his naked eye under a clear sky, the water smooth, when viewed through a telescope (his "perspective glass"), satisfied Finney in a moment as being, instead, "some aquatic animal, with the form, motion and appearance of which I had hitherto been unacquainted."

Finney estimated him to be about thirty feet long as he moved "with great rapidity" to the north for about a half mile, when suddenly the animal "turned about, and while turning, displayed a greater length than I had before seen; I supposed at least an hundred feet. It then came towards me, in a southerly direction very rapidly, until he was in line with me, when he stopped and lay entirely on the surface of the water."

Peering through his glass, Captain Finney described that the sea serpent's "appearance in this situation was like a string of buoys. I saw perhaps thirty or forty of these protuberances or bunches, which were about the size of a barrel." The head was about six or eight feet long, Finney said, and "where it was connected with the body was a little larger than the body," a head that "tapered off to the size of a horse's head" on which Finney could discern no mouth but a white stripe extending the whole length of his head just above the water under "what I supposed to be his under jaw."

Finney thought that the stretched-out serpent, which could remain still and motionless for five minutes or more, was 100 or 120 feet long but, unable to see anything that looked like its tail, he was not sure. "His colour was a deep brown or black," Finney said, "I could not discover any eyes, mane, gills or breathing holes. I did not see any fins or legs. The animal did not utter any sound, and it did not appear to notice anything."

The next morning, after a fresh breeze from the south subsided and all was calm, for about two hours, Finney watched again. He saw less of the animal's length. Finney never could discern whether its motion was "up and down or to the right and left" (horizontal or vertical, in terms of the committee's original question list) but, at its quickest, the animal plowed through the water somehow "at the rate of fifteen or twenty miles an hour" and, Finney noticed that morning, the sea serpent "often disappeared and was gone five or ten minutes underwater." Finney thought that he was "diving, or fishing for his food," the start of summer being the season during which "mackerel, menhaden, herring and other bait fish" come into Plymouth Bay in abundance.

His French target sailed into Judge Davis's sights. As a well-informed, patriotic American, Judge Davis's nostrils would have flared at the chance to smash the Buffon Argument. The late Count Buffon embodied the most arrogant of the scientific theories of the French authors of botanical and biological treatises, the one Jefferson kept in the forefront of his mind as a cultural challenge. Judge Davis must have savored his imminent Gloucester–Plymouth shot at the French *establissement*, as he, tongue-in-cheek and ironically, copied out quotes from French works at the Athenaeum, which he used exclusively as footnotes in his sea serpent text. Captain Finney's statement back from Plymouth, French footnotes in hand, Davis did a little more work in the library in order to quote from Pontoppidan, bishop of Bergen, in the *Natural History of Norway*, about a North Sea serpent that "continually keeps himself at the bottom of the sea, excepting in the months of July and August, which is their spawning time." He also received, apparently unsolicited, an annoying note from Reverend William Jenks of Bath, one of the Massachusetts Commissioners to the Indians (Maine became a separate state only in 1820; in 1817 it was still part of the Commonwealth of Massachusetts), something so stupid that the judge probably only included it as the gift of an old Federalist ally who was politically difficult to exclude from his book. Jenks's third-hand story told of how a sea serpent had sunk a ship by leaping between its masts and landing, smashing it to pieces, in Penobscot Bay. But all of the above, Pontoppidan and even Jenks's foolish story, being historical and recycled, were of nominal harm. The true source of danger to the committee wiggled in off-stage, the tempting little black snake of Loblolly Cove.

Judge Davis's good fortune had reached high tide.

Chapter 17

THE LOBLOLLY COVE SNAKE
BREAKS THE TIE

On September 28, 1817, Lonson Nash made the mistake of his life. He wrote a letter that, within a year, he would have given almost anything but Nabby and his children to take back. He sent Judge Davis an invitation to disaster.

Disguised as good news—great news!—Nash thought that there was something he had to tell Judge Davis immediately, a wonder of wonders. Although his agency had expired and he had been thanked for his services (apparently in person by the kiss of a pretty woman, as he wrote Judge Davis on September 9, that he was highly gratified not only by the society's vote of thanks but also "the agreeable manner, and respectable channel, through which their vote of thanks was communicated" to him), Nash went into full gear as the committee's agent without authority.

His invitation reached the judge at a vulnerable point.

With all of its material, the committee ought to have battened down the hatches and made straight for port. The ironic part of the crash was that the committee knew—everybody knew—that sample sea serpents were hard to find and harder to catch. For that reason, the original plan was to damn the specimen requirement and to go full speed with sequestered witnesses. No specimens but statements had been the plan: statements of reputable people signed on paper and sworn to before notaries. The scientific world would be left to deal with the obvious and excusable fact that the committee had no specimen of a hundred-foot, multi-ton, extremely fast and tremendously strong, swimming and diving champion. This was not a new daisy or an undiscovered butterfly.

And yet Judge Davis and his committee, their success so complete so quickly, their hubris set on high, were enchanted when Nash reported the Loblolly Cove specimen, even though Nash—their agent and the judge's friend—enjoined the committee that "the young serpent ought to undergo the severest scrutiny." Nash wrote in vain. Nash also cautioned the committee in vain that a Salem newspaper's article, that the sea serpent had itself been seen on the eastern shore at or near Loblolly Cove, was traceable to no source. Nash had dutifully sought out and spoke with its author, a Dr. Kittredge, who said that his source was rumor, a "general report," with no other evidence. Nash reminded the committee that the sea serpent was a "mammoth prodigy" and told them of his own mindset, that "I do not believe that he was ever seen on land here."

All of Nash's warnings were useless. He would be forever the Pandora who opened the box or, rather, packed the box to be shipped to Boston. The committee otherwise slapped together a four-page analysis adorned with three footnotes like amulets against disaster in French from both Daudin's and Lacepede's snake treatises. In the committee members' eyes, the Loblolly Cove baby resembled its Gloucester harbor parent and that was that. Nash's warning words were futile. The committee was swept away by its "baby sea serpent." All precautions previously taken were suddenly for naught: the depositions of sequestered witnesses who signed sworn statements; the uniform list of questions; the committee's own investigation when the *Laura* landed; and its rules, its discipline, its scholarship. Judge Davis and his committee ultimately put forth a land snake as a sea serpent specimen.

In fact, their "baby sea serpent" was a misshapen example of the black racer commonly found in New England. But this mutant reptile a yard long found on shore by a boy in Gloucester they presumed to name *Scoliophis atlanticus*, Latin for "Atlantic Humpty Serpent." Dissected by Dr. Bigelow and offered as the illustrated climax of their book, Humpty killed the committee's credibility. No one accepted a snake as the hatchling of an egg deposited in beach sand by a pregnant sea serpent. The public concluded that the emperor had no clothes. The proposed new species withered on the vine. Nobody lingered long over the statements. The committee's calculated, careful, rule-bound, structured and successful study of multiple sightings of the sea serpent incredibly misfired.

The committee's desire for a specimen overcame its scientific discipline. The members' shared knowledge included facts that the sea serpent was huge; that rapidity was his chief characteristic; that he left a quarter-mile wake as he cut through the seas; and that he was the most flexible of oceanic

The Loblolly Cove mutant black snake, pictured here, was probably drawn by Dr. Jacob Bigelow, a Harvard Medical School professor and gifted draftsman who served as the scientific consultant on Judge Davis's committee. Gloucester's justice of the peace, Lonson Nash, likely regretted having been the one who sent word to Judge Davis that this snake had been found and that locals believed it to be a baby sea serpent. *Courtesy of the Cape Ann Museum.*

beasts. The sea serpent regularly did four-minute miles. He was faster than a human being at full speed. Plymouth carpenters had emphasized the long wake of the creature they saw. But the committee was blind to the red flag in Nash's account. Neither Dr. Bigelow, the scientist who would draw the snake for the book, nor any other committee member found these facts fatally inconsistent with Nash's report that, while alive, the land snake's "progress was very slow, not near so fast as a man ordinarily walks."

Muffled drums.

Measured pace.

The death warrant of their project, signed by all committee members, read as follows:

> *On the whole, as these two animals agree in so many conspicuous, important and peculiar characters, and as no material difference between them has yet been clearly pointed out, excepting that of size; the Society will probably feel justified in considering them individuals of the same species, and entitled to the same name, until a more close examination of the great Serpent shall have disclosed some difference of structure, important enough to constitute a specific distinction.*

There was no closer examination of the snake by the committee or of Judge Davis's book by the scientific community. Scientists in France— scientists everywhere—rejected the book with its fold-out snake centerfold. They threw out the sea serpent along with the baby.

Chapter 18

IN THE SEA SERPENT'S WAKE

Up and down the North Shore, newspapers alone covered the second coming of the sea serpent in June 1819 when, between Lynn and Gloucester, hundreds of people saw a familiar figure: the sleek, the sociable, the speedy sea serpent! It frolicked outside the surf in deeper waters, a bit farther from witnesses than in Gloucester harbor in 1817. No sworn depositions were taken; no list of questions was circulated; Judge Davis, now head of the Massachusetts Historical Society, and Attorney Gray and Doctor Bigelow, had other things to do. Their original work, which was met by baffled indifference in all nations, discouraged hope of any better reaction to supplemental reports or a second, larger Linnaean product. The Linnaean Society did not stir. The frustrated gentlemen involved found themselves facing and living in what was, after all, an incurious world that was unwilling to see—a world married to the quotidian and blind to the extraordinary.

No specimen, no proof—a three-foot common snake that moved slower than a man could walk was not considered related to the bigger, faster animal. Buffon's theory was wrong; Buffon would be shown to be wrong, but the Davis committee was not the team that would show the world that Buffon was wrong. Where Jefferson had failed, so did Judge Davis. European theorists sailed on, with no wind knocked out of their sails. When attached to the snake, Nash's depositions were seen as ciphers, a long row of zeroes that still added up to zero.

Nevertheless, the book's technical consultant and illustrator may not have regretted his participation. The only glimpse we have of Dr.

Bigelow on the sea serpent after the book came out is like a silent movie with no captions. He did not want to rekindle thoughts about the sea serpent. That much is clear. Why he refused is unclear. The story is in a short memoir by a friend of Bigelow's, now in the collection of the Massachusetts Historical Society. When a gentleman and fellow scholar visited Dr. Bigelow many years after Judge Davis's book had been published and rejected, he hoped to question Bigelow "as to his *maturer* views about this sea-monster." Although they met under convivial circumstances, as soon as the visitor edged up on the topic with what he termed "prompting," he encountered resistance. Apparently the doctor winced or stiffened or an angel flew through the room, creating a sudden silence or abrupt and monosyllabic conversation. Something Bigelow's inquisitor did not clearly describe but clearly felt indicated the doctor's displeasure and demonstrated at the same time that committee members, in their "maturer years," were disinclined to revisit, redo or recant anything. The world had rejected their report but their collection of genuine observations of a marine animal unknown to science, a new species discovered in America by American citizens, still remained for anybody to see. Dr. Bigelow's silent stare or scowl or whatever before a friend in his parlor on the subject exposes pain persisting in him over the world's rejection of the sea serpent along with the Loblolly Cove snake. Dr. Bigelow seems to have died a believer in the sea serpent who felt that the book's rejection was undeserved.

Did Gloucester (apart from the eyewitnesses) embrace the sea serpent's story?

Gloucester's sole recorded reaction to Judge Davis's book is terse, troubling and troubled.

It is terse because it could hardly be terser.

It is troubling because not much can be made too clearly from a single biblical allusion.

It is troubled because its author is most clearly in a worried frame of mind.

The comment, undated, possibly penned into Judge Davis's book years after 1818, was probably by a Gloucester person. The front page of the copy of Judge Davis's book that the Cape Ann Museum possesses, the one with that terse comment, shows that it was presented to one Benjamin N. Coles by a friend whose name is less legible, making Benjamin N. Coles himself the most likely suspect to write it into his gift copy. At the very end of the sea serpent material, at the bottom of page 36, just before the account of the little black snake, appears, "See Amos 9:3."

What that quick entry lacks in pedigree can be more than made up for by audacious speculation. Caution need not halt our exploration, as Judge Davis himself may have said upon opening the package containing the snake.

Coles's (or someone else's!) homemade footnote was clearly a shot across the bow of a book headed into uncharted waters for science. It commands that any reader aboard check a verse of one of the Old Testament prophets.

No less and no more than that, the footnote implied that Coles reached for the Bible and, in the Bible, found that the sea serpent was the subject of the prophet Amos, who associated its appearance with God's judgment upon sinners who could hide but not avoid the serpent's tooth.

Amos 9:3 reads: "And though they hide themselves in the top of

> 36
>
> a point, but the body, which looks to be as big as two hogsheads, grows remarkably small at once just where the tail begins. The head in all the kinds has a high and broad forehead, but in some a pointed snout, though in others that is flat, like that of a cow or horse, with large nostrils, and several stiff hairs standing out on each side like whiskers. They add that the eyes of this creature are very large, of a blue colour, and look like a couple of bright pewter plates. The whole animal is of a dark brown colour, but it is speckled and variegated with light streaks or spots, that shine like tortoise shell. It is of a darker hue about the eyes and mouth than elsewhere, and appears in that part a good deal like those horses, which we call Moors heads.—Those on our coast differ from the Greenland sea snakes, with regard to the skin, which is as smooth as glass, and has not the least wrinkle but about the neck, where there is a kind of mane, which looks like a parcel of sea weeds hanging down to the water. Some say it sheds its skin like the land snake. It seems the wind is so destructive to this creature, that, as has been observed before, it is never seen on the surface of the water, but in the greatest calm, and the least gust of wind drives it immediately to the bottom again. These creatures shoot through the water like an arrow out of a bow, seeking constantly the coldest places. I have been informed by some of our seafaring men that a cable would not be long enough to measure the length of some of them, when they are observed on the surface of the water in an even line. They say those round lumps or folds sometimes lie one after another as far as a man can see."
>
> " If any one inquires how many folds may be counted in a Sea Snake, the answer is, that the number is not always the same, but depends upon the various sizes of them ; *five and twenty* is the greatest number I find well attested. Adam Olearius in his Gottorf Museum, p. 17. writes of it thus : " A person of distinction from Sweden related here at Gottorf, that he had heard the Burgomaster of Malmoe, a very worthy man, say, that as he was once standing on the top of a high hill towards the North Sea, he saw in the water, which was very calm, a Snake, which
>
> * See Amos 9:3.

Page 36 of Judge Davis's book. Note the margin comment, which refers to a biblical prophecy about sea serpents. *Courtesy of Cape Ann Museum.*

Carmel, I will search and take them out from thence; and though they be hid from my sight in the bottom of the sea, thence will I command the serpent, and he shall bite them."

By citing that verse, some representative of the Gloucester community made visible and preserved his awe before an animated instrument of the Lord, a denizen of the deep that normally hid from men's sight at the bottom of the sea, a deep sea creature known to Amos eating mackerel in Gloucester harbor, which was no more than eighty feet deep in any spot. Moreover, the prophesied creature had surfaced after an ominous year without a summer, shortly after the war that shook Gloucester to its church steeples, while people hid from harm until the erstwhile world conqueror Napoleon fell, as those not reading the Bible were reading about the cursed ancient mariner, the monster of Frankenstein and vampires and other nightmares.

The sea serpent was understood to be punitive. When Gaffney's shot failed, his failure was portentous; when the scientific committee stumbled, it was doubly so. As Gloucester preferred Amos's bottom line—that the sea serpent would bite and that there was no escape from the true judgment of the Lord, whether on land or sea, high or low—Gloucester witnessed as bullets bounced off, and Gaffney's one shot failed.

Bible believers knew, along with Amos, that the sea serpent was sent as God's sheepdog in water, sent to remind human beings not with its bark but with its bite to stay within human limits and to not think they were outside of God's power at anytime, anywhere. This sacred messenger had chosen the people of Gloucester to visit, people who looked at Judge Davis's book and then put it aside and continued to read their Bibles. They believed that their town was given the sea serpent to marvel at without capturing it or killing it, before the Lord took it away, and that Judge Davis's scientific interpretation, even before the pages in which the committee elevated a Loblolly Cove snake into the pantheon of Linnaean species, was not right.

The sea serpent was a mystery and, as Lewis Hyde once noted, "mystery" comes from the Greek word *muein*, meaning to close one's mouth. "Dictionaries tend to explain the connection," Hyde wrote, "by pointing out that the initiates to ancient mysteries were sworn to silence, but the root may also indicate, it seems to me, that what the initiate learns at a mystery *cannot* be talked about. It can be shown, it can be written or revealed, it cannot be explained."

In reaction to the judge's scientific report, "See Amos 9:3" says it all. It says that, if you want to know about the sea serpent, do not read Judge Davis's book, but look at the sea serpent, read the Bible and be silent.

So it would seem to an onlooker that science was packing up its tent and moving out of New England, chastened. As Judge Davis's book failed, the Linnaean Society of New England over which Judge Davis had presided dissolved. Hopes high, it had applied for a corporate charter and was granted one in 1820, but by 1822, its members voted to "suspend meetings." Their sorry, dusty collection of specimens went first to be neglected by Harvard, then transferred to a private museum in Boston until what remained passed on to the Museum of Science in 1948.

Gloucester people would have kept a wary, prophetic eye open on poor Lonson Nash, who had, in their presence, more than any person, expropriated the sacred sea serpent for secular purposes.

Never again did Nash serve as senator or representative.

Before the end of the 1820s, there was no Federalist Party in Massachusetts. The party ended before Nash left the party. Within a half-dozen years of the sea serpent sightings and his depositions, Justice Lonson Nash, friend of Judge Davis and dashing associate of Blue Light Federalists who had dreamed once of seceding and creating their own country, was serving as the town's humble schoolmaster. In 1824, Nash became the teacher of Gloucester's one-room grammar school, towering over benches of nervous young scholars as they recited their lessons or scraped arithmetic on their slate boards. Either Nash felt a sudden, intense urge to teach or, more likely, at age forty-four, the college graduate who practiced law was simply fitted for few other jobs available in Gloucester.

After 1824, his one year as teacher, no records account for almost thirty lost years, years of public obscurity and presumed forms of involuntary penance. Nabby and her Lonny's two daughters never married but earned their keep (or supported their parents) as maiden schoolteachers. At some point, probably the late 1840s, Nash lost even the consolation of Nabby's companionship, after which he put his name in for Essex County commissioner of insolvency, a position he secured, in which he worked with creditors, down-and-out merchants and the disabled and elderly people who had fallen into hard times. It was the last public office he filled. Likely without regret, although his married son, grandchildren and his two daughters continued to live in Gloucester—his own home for over fifty years—Nash returned to the Berkshires from whence he had come long before, once when he was a rising, young Federalist about to fall in love.

Nash died on February 10, 1863, in Great Barrington.

Although in 1863 there had been no Federalist Party for forty years, Nash seemed still to have defended and praised Federalist policies for decades, perhaps loudly and crankily, because the Essex County lawyers who knew him, in their short memorial, described Nash politically as "a member of the old Federal party, to which he was strongly attached while that party existed," with no indication that he ever adopted any other party rather than remain a political orphan. His fellow lawyers were unaware of his naturalization. Apparently, Nash never spoke much about his family or his presumed British birth. Assuming an ancient American ancestry, his fellow lawyers worded their memorial resolution formulaically that Nash had wanted "to spend his few remaining years in the scenes of his childhood and the home of his fathers."

Another man thought that Gloucester lawyers should die in Gloucester. In John Babson's history of Gloucester, he scowled in a footnote that Gloucester lawyers rarely lived in Gloucester and never died in it! Babson—who wrote in the 1860s, knew Nash and whose pages refer to many of Nash's sunnier moments and political successes—probably thought ill of Nash's having left

Where once a 150-foot sea serpent played, today a long breakwater stretches out from Eastern Point, insulating the harbor from storms. *Courtesy of Manuel Simoes.*

town to die in the Berkshires. If Gloucester's historian, a Babson of the Babson family that went back to Gloucester's original settlement, fondly wished that Nash, a good old fellow for all he was a diehard Federalist, should have found his final resting place in the town that the sea serpent visited, that was, indeed, local tribute of a high order.

Buried in Gloucester or not, Nash left a living legacy. His joint product with Judge Davis, Dr. Bigelow and Attorney Gray—the sea serpent book— was the rosy-fingered dawn of people's science in the United States, of the observations of ordinary men and women being judged worthy of publication. Justice Nash cast as wide a net as his Federalist principles allowed him to interview people all of whose roots were outside of academia, who lacked scientific training and whose sheer, interested observation of nature constituted the record he was charged to preserve. We have their specific, detailed and perceptive sightings because Nash took pains to make careful records of their words.

No one in Gloucester ever hinted that there was any kind of a hoax or mistaken identification. And statements sworn to before Justice Nash were never retracted. Instead, when those eight Gloucester men gave sworn statements before Justice Nash, in pledging their souls and jeopardizing their

This schooner "scoons" past Hammond Castle at about the spot where a legendary pair of ladies (maybe) saw the sea serpent quietly enter Gloucester harbor on August 6, 1817. The same spot was, in the 1930s, the scene of John Hays Hammond's experiments in remote control. *Courtesy of Manuel Simoes.*

eternal lives, they literally bet their salvation on having seen a sea serpent. If hoax it was, it was one hell of a hoax!

Science in America marched on and had little to do with Gloucester for many years. Enter Yale graduate John Hays Hammond Jr., the eccentric genius who built Hammond Castle overlooking Gloucester harbor but was largely a self-educated inventor. Remote control was his thing. In the 1930s, by using his prototype device on an unoccupied speedboat and controlling the boat by radio from shore, Hammond did his work almost exactly to the very wave where the sea serpent of Gloucester was first spotted in 1817.

It was as if the world in a little more than a century had gone full circle.

The living dinosaurs were dead; long live the human beings!

A double-exposure photograph of the sea serpent over Hammond's speedboat would reflect how, in Gloucester harbor, the primordial creature of 1817 had been lately succeeded. Notwithstanding the dire predictions of Amos 9:3, in which the sea serpent was to have had the last bite, the most adaptable species on earth—the species that saw and described the sea serpent of 1817, as Nash recorded—had found its floundering, jerky way to make further progress. "The Man at the Wheel" in Gloucester was succeeded by the man not at the wheel. Literally in the path of the sea serpent, the man not at the wheel reversed biblical prophecy and went down to the sea in unmanned submarines to the lowest depths and higher than Mount Carmel in rockets to the moon and to the stars.

In the end, neither Amos nor the critics of Nash's work and of Judge Davis's book have the last word. Nash, who loved the woman of his life too well to leave Gloucester while she still lived; Nash, the industrious scribe, whose work was taken for nonsense by many in his lifetime and who exemplifies a perfect dedication to truth over any opposition and ridicule and despite all setbacks; Nash, the noble, old Federalist who was destroyed for being a peace activist and who soldiered on in obscurity without the rewards of either fame or fortune—if only unconsciously, in applying the scientific method to observations in Gloucester harbor, Hammond followed Nash. And so, not in irony but in sincere salute, the last words of this book are, thus: Hurrah for Nash!

BIBLIOGRAPHY

Babson, John J. *History of the Town of Gloucester, Cape Anne, including the Town of Rockport.* Gloucester, MA: Proctor Brothers, 1860.

Bedini, Silvio A. *Thomas Jefferson, Statesman of Science.* New York: Macmillan Publishing Company, 1990.

Cohn, Marjorie B. *Francis Calley Gray and Art Collecting for America.* Cambridge, MA: Harvard University Press, 1986.

Conniff, Richard. "All-American Monsters," *Smithsonian* 41, no. 1, (April 2010), 38.

Davis, John, Francis C. Gray and Jacob Bigelow, MD. *Report of a Committee of the Linnaean Society of New England relative to a Large Marine Animal, Supposed to be a Serpent, Seen near Cape Ann, Massachusetts, in August, 1817.* Boston: privately published, 1818. (Copy available at the Cape Ann Museum, Gloucester, Massachusetts.)

Davis, William T. *Bench and Bar of the Commonwealth of Massachusetts.* Boston: Boston History Co., 1895.

Dugatkin, Lee Alan. *Mr. Jefferson and the Giant Moose; Natural History in Early America.* Chicago: University of Chicago Press, 2009.

Grant, James. "The Rise of Juristocracy," *The Wilson Quarterly* (Spring 2010), 16–22.

Heuvelmans, Bernard. *In the Wake of Sea-Serpents.* New York: Hill and Wang, 1968.

Lindholdt, Paul J., ed. *John Josselyn, Colonial Traveler; A Critical Edition of Two Voyages to New-England*. Hanover, NH: University Press of New England, 1988.

Miller, Charles A. *Jefferson and Nature, An Interpretation*. Baltimore: The Johns Hopkins University Press, 1988.

O'Brien, Michael. *Mrs. Adams in Winter; A Journey in the Last Days of Napoleon*. New York: Farrar, Straus and Giroux, 2010.

O'Neill, J.P. "The Great New England Sea Serpent." 1999. http://www.pibburns.com/tgness.htm.

Wikipedia. Attorney Francis C. Gray. http://www.wikipedia.org.

————. Dr. Jacob Bigelow.

————. Harvard College.

————. Judge John Davis.

————. Linnaean Society of New England.

ABOUT THE AUTHOR

 Wayne Soini was born in Gloucester in 1948, regrettably too late to see the sea serpent swim into or out of the harbor. He graduated from Gloucester High School in 1966. His most recent degree, a master's degree in history from the University of Masssachusetts–Boston, was awarded in 2009. Soini coauthored the biographical sketch and local sports history book *Judge Fuchs and the Boston Braves*, with the late Robert Fuchs in 1998. Soini is a member of the National Writers Union, Local 1981, Boston Chapter, and of the Boston Athenaeum. He makes his living as a lawyer and lives with his partner, Anne, in Brookline, where he basically reads and watches his weight. (Mostly, he watches it increase.)

Visit us at
www.historypress.net